The History of the Blues

Andy Koopmans
AR B.L.: 9.9
Points: 5.0   UG

The Music
Library

The History
of the Blues

Other books in this series include:

The Music Library

The History of the Blues

by Andy Koopmans

LUCENT BOOKS
An imprint of Thomson Gale, a part of The Thomson Corporation

THOMSON ™

GALE

Detroit • New York • San Francisco • San Diego • New Haven, Conn. • Waterville, Maine • London • Munich

To all those who made the blues what it is.

LIBRARY OF CONGRESS CATALOGING-IN-PUBLICATION DATA

Koopmans, Andy.
  The history of the blues / by Andy Koopmans.
    p. cm. — (The music library)
  Includes bibliographical references (p.   ) and index.
  ISBN 1-59018-767-9 (hard cover : alk. paper)
  1. Blues (Music)—History and criticism—Juvenile literature. I. Title. II. Series: Music library (San Diego, Calif.)
  ML3521.K67 2005
  781.643'09—dc22
                                                                    2005009784

Printed in the United States of America

• Contents •

• Foreword •

In the nineteenth century English novelist Charles Kingsley wrote, "Music speaks straight to our hearts and spirits, to the very core and root of our souls. . . . Music soothes us, stirs us up . . . melts us to tears." As Kingsley stated, music is much more than just a pleasant arrangement of sounds. It is the resonance of emotion, a joyful noise, a human endeavor that can soothe the spirit or excite the soul. Musicians can also imitate the expressive palate of the earth, from the violent fury of a hurricane to the gentle flow of a babbling brook.

The word *music* is derived from the fabled Greek muses, the children of Apollo who ruled the realms of inspiration and imagination. Composers have long called upon the muses for help and insight. Music is not merely the result of emotions and pleasurable sensations, however.

Music is a discipline subject to formal study and analysis. It involves the juxtaposition of creative elements such as rhythm, melody, and harmony with intellectual aspects of composition, theory, and instrumentation. Like painters mixing red, blue, and yellow into thousands of colors, musicians blend these various elements to create classical symphonies, jazz improvisations, country ballads, and rock-and-roll tunes.

Throughout centuries of musical history, individual musical elements have been blended and modified in infinite ways. The resulting sounds may convey a whole range of moods, emotions, reactions, and messages. Music, then, is both an expression and reflection of human experience and emotion.

The foundations of modern musical styles were laid down by the first ancient musicians who used wood, rocks, animal skins—and their own bodies—to recreate the sounds of the natural world in which they lived. With their hands, their feet, and their very breath they ignited the passions of listeners and moved them to their feet. The dancing, in turn, had a mesmerizing and hypnotic effect that allowed people to transcend their worldly concerns. Through music they could achieve a level of shared experience that could not be found in other forms of communication. For this reason, music has always been part of religious endeavors, from ancient Egyptian religious ceremonies to modern Christian masses. And it has inspired dance movements from kings and queens spinning the minuet to punk rockers slamming together in a mosh pit.

By examining musical genres ranging from Western classical music to rock and roll, readers will find a new understanding of old music and develop an appreciation for new sounds. Books in Lucent's Music Library focus on the music, the musicians, the instruments, and on music's place in cultural history. The songs and artists examined may be easily found in the CD and sheet music collections of local libraries so that readers may study and enjoy the music covered in the books. Informative sidebars, annotated bibliographies, and complete indexes highlight the text in each volume and provide young readers with many opportunities for further discussion and research.

The Music of Survival

If someone feels down, despondent, filled with sadness and melancholy, one might say that he or she has the blues. The English language abounds with expressions associating emotions with color: One can be green with envy or purple with rage. For centuries, the color blue has been associated with sadness. By the mid-nineteenth century, the expression "the blues" was commonly used in this way. For example, in 1846, while fighting in the Mexican-American War, a depressed young soldier named Ulysses S. Grant—who would go on to become the eighteenth president of the United States—wrote in a letter to his wife, "I came back to my tent and to drive away what you call the Blues, I took up some of your old letters."[1]

Throughout the history of America, having the blues was a common feeling for many black Americans. During slavery and in the years that followed emancipation, African Americans experienced daily hardship as they struggled to survive in a country where they were confronted with racism, violence, and poverty. As one bluesman said, "You been troubled, you been broke, you been hungry, no job no money. The one you loved deserted you. That makes you blue."[2]

Around the turn of the twentieth century, African Americans expressed these feelings of sadness in a music unlike any that had been heard before in America. Rising out of the Deep South, the music became known as the blues. It was an original American folk art that, like Native American music, is believed to be among the only original roots music to be born in the United States.

Songs of Heartache

Tonally, the blues was simple, most often using only three musical chords per song. However, the chords included so-called blue notes, which fell outside the standard European musical scale but corresponded to the African vocal scale. These notes gave the blues its signature strained, melancholy tone.

This melancholy tone helped blues musicians express their stories, and even today almost every blues song is a story, however loosely it is told. As legendary blues guitarist B.B. King notes, the blues is about the world: "It's the music of people, places, and things."[3] And the narrative of the blues is about how that world has mistreated the singer. He or she sings about misfortune, hardship, and struggle so common to African American life at the time the blues was

In this 1940 photo, legendary blues musicians Honey Hill (left) and Big Bill Broonzy (right) pose with their guitars, with piano player Memphis Slim in the center.

born. In 1941 African American poet and writer Langston Hughes wrote about this struggle:

The blues are folk-songs born out of heartache . . . out of black, beaten, but unbeatable throats. . . . [They are] *today* songs, here and now, broke and broken-hearted, when you're troubled in mind and don't know what to do and nobody cares. . . . There are the family Blues, when a man and woman have quarreled, and the quarrel can't be patched up. There's the loveless blues, when you haven't even got anybody to quarrel with. And there's the left-lonesome Blues, when the one you care for's gone away. Then there's also the broke-and-hungry Blues, a stranger in a strange town. . . .[4]

However, despite its sad lyrics and tones, for most people, the blues is not a depressing music because it finds light in the darkest places. As Hughes continues, "For sad as Blues may be, there's almost always something humorous about them—even if it's the kind of humor that laughs to keep from crying."[5]

It is this laughter in the face of sadness that many say made the blues so important in the lives of so many downtrodden people. The blues helped sus-

The Rolling Stones is just one of the countless artists whose sound is strongly influenced by American blues.

tain people through their troubles, and in doing so helped them survive. As blues historian Max Haymes writes,

For above all else, the blues is a music of survival. . . . [A listener] can draw on an almost unassailable feeling of solidarity with the rest of the black community. This inner strength helps develop a central philosophy of the Blues, which sustains an individual throughout their life.[6]

Influence of the Blues

Many scholars and critics believe that it is because of the blues's ability to uplift and strengthen people's will and to create solidarity that it has grown and lasted for more than a century. As folk historian Alan Lomax writes, this is because the blues has become widely relevant in the modern world:

All of us are beginning to experience the melancholy dissatisfaction that weighed upon the hearts of black people [when the blues began]. . . . Feelings of anomie and alienation, of orphaning and rootlessness—the sense of being a commodity rather than a person; the loss of love and of family and of place—this modern syndrome was the norm for the [founders of the blues] a hundred years ago. . . . Our species has never been more powerful or wealthy, nor more ill at ease. Homeless and desperate people in America and all over the world live in the shadow of undreamed-of productivity and luxury.[7]

Additionally, the blues has had a strong influence on virtually all American popular music, imbuing other genres as diverse as country, rock, jazz, and hip-hop with its thematic, rhythmic, and tonal qualities. The blues's focus on everyday life and problems, for example, has become the foundation of modern lyrics, just as derivations of its strong rhythmic backbeat and wailing guitar strains are commonplace to most popular music.

For more than a century, the blues has transformed itself again and again. However, as it has spread and influenced other genres of music, it has never given up its basic simplicity, honesty, and rhythm. In the strains of even contemporary blues, there are echoes of its earliest traditions and influences.

Chapter One

The Origins of the Blues

While the exact details about the origins of the blues are uncertain, it is clear that it evolved from the meeting of two distinct experiences. African traditions, instruments, and folklore combined with the conditions blacks experienced in the Deep South during slavery—and especially in the period of continued violence, oppression, and hardship that followed emancipation—to produce a kind of music never heard before.

For more than two centuries the institution of slavery had repressed blacks in America. Emancipation, which came in 1863, and the Union victory in the Civil War in 1865 offered African Americans hope for a better life. Even with the end of slavery, however, hardship remained a daily experience for African Americans. The promises of a better life were crushed by violence, escalating racism, and laws structured to keep them from ever attaining full citizenship in the country that they had helped to build. It was during this period of disappoint-

ment, bitterness, and anger that the blues would be created.

Slavery

The first Africans arrived in the United States in 1619, and for the next 250 years, approximately 15 million Africans were brought to the Americas as slaves. It was the largest forced migration in human history, and it dramatically changed the lives of both the slaves and the culture into which they came.

At first, the African slave population was concentrated in the rural areas of Maryland, Virginia, the Carolinas, and Georgia, because these were the areas in which their physical labor was most needed to plant, tend, and harvest the agricultural cash crops of tobacco and cotton. However, with the invention of the cotton gin in 1793, cotton became an extremely profitable crop in the Deep South. Mechanization of the textile industry in the United States had so dramatically increased the demand for cotton that farmers could not keep up with production until the cotton gin made it possible to rapidly clean cotton. The gin separated the useful cotton fiber from its seeds at a much more rapid rate than could be done by hand. With production speeds increasing, demand for more cotton-growing land rose sharply, and farmers expanded into the territory west of the Appalachian Mountains. With these farmers went their labor force of slaves, who were still needed to work the fields.

The Louisiana Purchase of 1803 also opened a vast expanse of land beyond the Mississippi River to the west. During this period, farmers and their slaves moved into the regions of what would become Alabama, Mississippi, Tennessee, Arkansas, Louisiana, and east Texas. During the nineteenth century, this region was densely populated with slaves and a large black culture developed. Out of this region and this culture grew new styles of African American music based on African traditions.

African Traditions

In Africa, music and dance were important and basic parts of everyday life. Music was used in work, and both dance and music were employed in religious and social events. In America they remained important to the African and African American people.

Upon arrival in America, tribes and even families were split up, and slaves

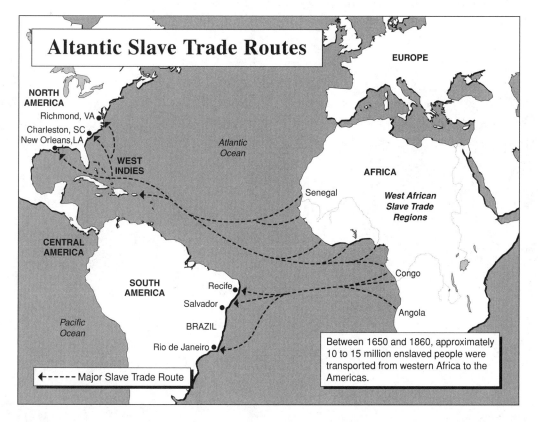

Altantic Slave Trade Routes

EUROPE

NORTH AMERICA

Richmond, VA

Charleston, SC

New Orleans, LA

Atlantic Ocean

WEST INDIES

AFRICA

Senegal

West African Slave Trade Regions

CENTRAL AMERICA

Congo

SOUTH AMERICA

Recife

Salvador

BRAZIL

Angola

Pacific Ocean

Rio de Janeiro

Between 1650 and 1860, approximately 10 to 15 million enslaved people were transported from western Africa to the Americas.

←----- Major Slave Trade Route

from different tribes who spoke different languages were often thrown together to keep them from uniting and uprising against their enslavers. Under these circumstances, music and dance were vital to their survival. It helped alleviate the loneliness, isolation, and alienation most suffered. It helped them communicate, kept them company, and lifted their spirits.

African Instruments

African instruments came to America along with African slaves between the seventeenth and nineteenth centuries. Over time, many of these instruments were adapted and became important components of African American music.

Slave traders customarily allowed instruments on their slave ships so that the Africans could dance and get exercise during the long crossing. For most of the journey from the west coast of Africa to the eastern seaboard of the United States, slaves were kept chained and crowded together belowdecks in dark, hot, suffocating conditions. Slave traders arranged for them to get exercise by dancing on deck in the fresh air, hoping it would prevent them from falling into depression and dying. It would also keep them healthier and thus

This nineteenth-century engraving depicts a slave auction in the New World. Separated from their families, slaves often turned to music and dance as a source of solace.

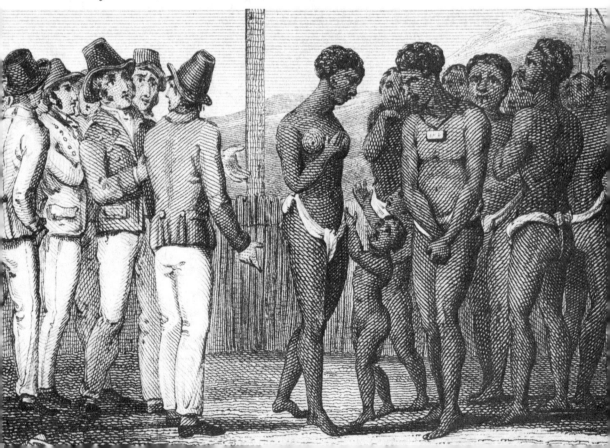

Transplanting African Musical Traditions

In their March 1991 article in the UNESCO Courier, *journalists Etienne Bours and Alberto Nogueira explore the origins of contemporary American music in the African traditions brought to America during slavery. In this excerpt, they discuss how features of African culture were changed, destroyed, or adapted by this transplanting of traditions.*

"We might be called a people of dancers, musicians and poets, since important events such as a triumphant return from war or any other reason for popular rejoicing, are celebrated by dancing accompanied by appropriate music and singing," wrote Olaudah Equiano, an Ibo slave taken to Virginia in 1756. These celebrations were not always tolerated. As a rule, the black slaves in Latin America lived in relatively closed communities and were able to preserve some tribal customs as well as their traditional rites and ceremonies. . . .

In contrast, the slaves who were transported to the United States via the Caribbean, where some features of their African culture were modified or obliterated, had to live in fairly close contact with their white owners. All their ancestral beliefs and means of self-expression were affected from the start. In the despair of captivity they clung to their cults, but practiced them in secret. . . . Although certain beliefs were expressed through a veil of symbolism, or through the fervent singing of spirituals, other African gods were worshipped in the open air, in the depths of the Mississippi bayous—as in the case of the Vaudou cult, known as Hoodoo in the southern United States. Secular music, on the other hand, was forced to comply with new functions in a new environment that was hostile to African traditions. All that survived were songs and dances that were compatible with the economic and social structure of the New World, such as the work songs ("field hollers"), born of African call and response chants, which allowed the slaves to pace their work and keep the overseer's whip at bay. The slaves could also use their talents to entertain their masters. Many of them played the fiddle, fife or drums. More than one escaped slave sought by his owner was described as an excellent singer or a skilled fiddle-player.

more valuable when sold in America. For this purpose, musical instruments familiar to the slaves were brought along. One trader said, "In the intervals between their meals [the slaves] are encouraged to divert themselves with music and dancing; for which purpose such rude and uncouth instruments as are used in Africa, are collected before their departure."[8]

The instruments brought on ships from Africa came from various regions of western Africa, including Senegal, Guinea, Gambia, and Nigeria. These included lutes, which were stringed instruments with a body shaped like a pear sliced lengthwise and a neck attached at the top. Strings made from plant fibers were attached at the base and neck, and could be tightened or loosened for tuning. The one-string lute (called a *riti* or *nyanyaur* by natives of Gambia) was played with a bow, while the two-stringed lute (called a *xalam* by natives of Senegal) was plucked. From the Sudan region also came the *goge*, which was a one-stringed fiddle that could be plucked or played with a bow.

Scholars believe that African expertise in these lute transferred to the European-style violin, which later became an important instrument in African American music.

Banjo

Another similar African lute used by the slaves was the bandore. The body of the instrument was made of a large, hollow gourd with a long handle or neck attached to it. It was strung with four or five strands of catgut, which were plucked to play the instrument. The slaves pronounced the instrument's name *banjar,* and the word eventually entered the English language as "banjo," the instrument still widely played today. As then-governor of Virginia and slave owner Thomas Jefferson noted in his 1781 book *Notes on the State of Virginia,* the banjo was also the origin of the guitar: "The instrument proper to [slaves] is the Banjar, which they brought hither from Africa, and which is the original of the guitar, its chords being precisely the four lower chords of the guitar."[9]

For the period up until the Civil War, the banjo and fiddle (or violin) became the predominant instruments in African American music. These would gradually be replaced by the guitar and harmonica in the years following the war.

Wind Instruments and Drums

In addition to the stringed instruments from Africa, flutes, horns, and drums were brought over. Wind instruments such as flutes and horns were made of wood or sometimes ivory and could be played in various tones that mimicked speech. This allowed people to communicate when they were far apart or to call animals while hunting. They were also used for ceremonial purposes, to talk to the gods or to represent the voices of their ancestors. African leaders also used wind instruments to let people know where they were, and as emblems of authority. For some African cultures, such as that of the Benin in West Africa, the horn was a symbol associated with war or processions.

Drums were equally essential to African life. Most Africans used music as part of their ceremonial religious life, and it was closely bound to the spiritual and supernatural world. On a practical level, it was used to motivate workers in the fields in the largely agricultural daily life of Africa. These agricultural activities, such as hoeing and chopping, were dependent on rhythm, which was provided by drums. Like wind instruments, drums were also used as a form of communication in rural communities by creating sounds that imitated the sounds of words in many African languages.

However, white owners attempted to strip African traditions from slaves upon their arrival in America. This often included their instruments, particularly horns and drums. In most areas (and later in states and territories), slaves were forbidden to possess these instruments because they were known to be used in communication, and slave owners feared they would

Drums have historically been at the center of African tribal life. Here, tribesmen in the former Belgian Congo beat drums during a religious celebration.

be used to start insurrections. This fear was so serious that a slave found with a horn or drum risked being executed. Only in New Orleans were drums and horns tolerated—a fact that would contribute to the development of a unique style of jazz and blues in New Orleans in the twentieth century.

Despite the efforts of their captors and owners to strip away their African identities, slaves retained their nature, dress, customs, language, music, and songs. Slaves improvised instruments similar to those from Africa. For instance, empty washbasins, sticks, quills, spoons, or animal bones could be used instead of drums for percussion. Further, percussion could be made by the body. Songs often included repetition of the same rhythms and phrases to make dance possible, and the dancers would stomp and clap in time to the music to provide the beat. For instance, in a type of dance called patting juba, slaves would rhythmically strike their hands on their knees, then clap their hands together, and then slap one shoulder then the other in time with the music.

African Language and Instruments

In Deep Blues, *Robert Palmer describes the connection between African communication, language, and music. In the following excerpt, he explains why most African slaves were deprived of instruments such as drums and horns when they were brought to America out of fear the slaves might use them to orchestrate escapes or revolts.*

M any . . . African peoples speak pitch-tone languages in which a single syllable or word has several meanings, and one indicates the desired meaning by speaking at an appropriate pitch level, usually high, middle, or low. Among these people, speech has melodic properties, and the melodies found in music suggest words and sentences. By using generally understood correspondences between pitch configurations in speech and in music, musicians can make their instruments talk. . . .

The use of musical instruments for signaling is found everywhere, and drummers learn rhythms by imitating either meaningful verbal phrases or onomatopoeic nonsense syllables. . . .

Singing

In African music, the voice was more important than any other instrument, including drums, and it was the one instrument that slave owners could not take away. Over time, slaves developed unique vocal techniques that were a blend of African and American styles. Singers used grunts, groans, and screams in their music to express emotion and frequently shortened or lengthened words to fit the rhythm of their music. They also employed so-called blue notes, which were tones from the African vocal scale that fell outside the traditional Western musical scale and could not be played on a piano. These notes were important contributors to African American music. In fact, it was because the guitar and harmonica were able to replicate these blue notes better than the banjo and the fiddle that the former instruments became more popular in African American music in the late nineteenth century.

African vocal tradition also involved antiphony, a technique in which a lyric or sound is sung out and then answered back, by another singer, group of singers, or the sound of an instrument. This alternation between leader and chorus, often termed call-and-response, is a defining characteristic of African music and became an important element of African American music, including the early songs sung by slaves while working in the fields.

Oral Tradition

Vocal music was a descendant of the oral traditions practiced by many African tribes. Many of these tribes relied on stories and songs as a means of passing on their history, religious beliefs, and culture.

In western Africa, a caste of storytellers called griots were extremely important because they carried on the history of their people. The role of griot (rhymes with "trio") was handed down from father to son for generations, and it was an honored and feared profession. Griots were elders of a tribe, honored because they were entertainers and important historians; they were feared because they often retaliated against those who angered them by spreading elaborate insults about the offender. A griot would tell his tales to groups of his people, often accompanying his story with an instrument called a *shekere,* which is a dried gourd, hollowed and closely wrapped in a net of beaded twine. The sound of the *shekere,* shaken or thumped, accompanied and punctuated the griot's voice.

In America, musicians often took on the unofficial position of griot, carrying stories about history and culture in the words of their songs. Like the griots in western Africa, the musicans used instruments to accompany their tales. This tradition was carried on in African American culture during slavery and after emancipation and was taken up by itinerant musicians at the turn of the twentieth century. These musicians told musical stories and in effect carried on much of the African American culture in their songs.

A group of slaves in Virginia gathers around a man as he sings and plays the banjo in this 1876 engraving.

Field Hollers, Jump-ups, and Work Songs

Of course, there were few if any professional musicians among slaves. Rather, they were laborers, and their music grew out of their daily life of work. Slaves on plantations were usually divided into two groups—house workers, who cared for the plantation owner's home and family, and field workers, who did all the work involved in raising and harvesting crops. It is from the field workers that hollers, jump-ups, and work songs developed.

Hollers were shouts—often not even words but sounds such as hoots or wails—bellowed from worker to worker across fields as a form of communication. Jump-ups were rhythmic one-line phrases, often about the worker's feelings or activity, that he or she sang out while working or dancing. Work songs were similar to jump-ups, but longer. Most work songs were sung to the rhythm of the work being performed; such as the beat of a sledgehammer striking rock or an axe hitting a tree. For example:

No more [beat] my Lord [beat]
No more [beat] my Lord [beat]
Lord I'll never [beat] turn back
[beat] no more [beat].[10]

In Africa it was typical for workers to sing while they worked in the fields. The songs they sang helped workers keep the rhythm of their work, and also served to keep the workers going and help the time go by. Whereas in Africa the songs had been happy ones, field songs in America were adapted to suit the harsh conditions of slaves, forced to work another man's land for no money. As in most African American music, the lyrics were improvisational and evolved to reflect the toil and pain of slavery, the hardship and boredom of work, and the loneliness of being separated from family and home. As author Marta J. Effinger writes, "Work songs . . . are protests against brutality. The oppressed slave, prisoner, and/or laborer share their experiences in work songs."[11]

These hollers and songs of laborers often carried secret meanings that whites were neither able nor meant to understand. During slave times, they were used by blacks coordinating escape or rebellion; in later years, they were often used as a safe way to speak out against oppressive conditions, mean or crooked landlords, and other injustices.

Prison Chain Gangs

In the years following emancipation, the group work songs of slaves were often replaced by another communal type of

A slave family harvests cotton on a Georgia plantation in the 1860s. Slaves often sang as a way to cope with their impossibly harsh working conditions.

song: the prison chain gang song. Some former plantations in the Deep South were converted into penal farms or penitentiaries, also known as "pens." The prisoners in these institutions were predominantly black and were routinely put to work doing tasks formerly accomplished by slaves.

Prisoners were chained together to keep them from running away, and in the Deep South it was common to see long lines of men in striped prison fatigues with shackles around their ankles digging trenches, breaking up rocks to gravel a road, or doing some other hard-labor task under the hot sun. As the agricultural workers had done in the fields, these men sang as they worked, keeping time with the rhythm of their tools.

Ballads

Closely related to the agricultural workers' songs and prison songs were ballads, which were essentially stories set to music. Like the ancient African griots, African American songsters used music to recount stories about great heroes and villains of the day. One of the more popular ballad figures was John Henry, a black man of amazing strength who worked digging tunnels on the railway line for the Chesapeake and Ohio Railroad. Based on an allegedly true story from the 1870s, one of the ballads told of John Henry challenging his white work-crew captain to let him race a steam drill in the digging of a massive tunnel, using only his hammer against the machine. As the song recounts,

A prison chain gang in 1937 labors under the watchful eye of an armed guard. Like field workers, chain gangs routinely sang as they worked.

John Henry said to his captain:
You are nothing but a common
  man,
Before that steam drill shall beat
  me down,
I'll die with my hammer in my
  hand. [12]

In some versions, John Henry dies while digging. However, as Effinger writes, such ballads still comforted people. She writes, "Like the spirituals, John Henry ballads are survival stories because the songs validate a people as they struggle through hardship." [13]

Spirituals

Another form of early black music that helped African Americans struggle through daily adversity was the spiritual. Spirituals were frequently tunes from Christian church hymns that had been modified and influenced by African traditions.

The church was one of the few places blacks were able to turn to with their problems, and thus it became a strong force in the African American community. Many slaves had been converted to Christianity during the eighteenth and nineteenth centuries by slave owners who tried to destroy traditional religious and supernatural beliefs such as animism and voodoo. They also believed that Christianized slaves would be easier to control through biblical lessons of obedience and determinism—the belief that everything is determined by God and there is no free will. Christianity became an essential theme in African American music.

However, even though most slaves converted to Christianity, they found their own empowering lessons from the Bible, closely identifying themselves with the Old Testament Hebrews, who had also been oppressed and enslaved. African American slaves incorporated these Christian stories into mournful spirituals, which, like work songs, were both expressive and comforting. One of the best known was "Go Down Moses," the lyrics of which recalled the story of Exodus 8:1, in which Moses, the leader of the Hebrews, demanded the Egyptian pharaoh release his people from slavery:

When Israel was in Egypt's Land,
Let my people go,
Oppressed so hard they could not
  stand,
Let my people go.
Chorus
Go down, Moses,
Way down in Egypt's Land.
Tell ol' Pharoah,
Let my people go.

Thus saith the Lord, bold Moses
  said,
Let my people go,
If not, I'll smite your first-born dead,
Let my people go.
[Repeat] *Chorus*

No more shall they in bondage toil,
Let my people go,
Let them come out with Egypt's
  spoil,
Let my people go.
[Repeat] *Chorus* [14]

Spirituals remained an important form of black music after emancipation as well, as the hardships of slavery were replaced by another system of violence and oppression: segregation.

Segregation and Hardship

Though free, in the late nineteenth century southern blacks found themselves up against discriminatory and segregationist Jim Crow laws. These laws allowed southern governments to con-

Separation and Isolation

Following slavery, African Americans suffered separation and isolation because their entire race was criminalized by whites who exploited their labor as prisoners. In this excerpt from his essay in the Spring 2001 Midwest Quarterly, *"From Down South to Up South: An Examination of Geography in the Blues," historian Hiram Nall discusses this separation and isolation.*

The reenslavement of African Americans after Emancipation finds expression in blues lyrics that give voice to the isolation and separation that resulted. As large numbers of African Americans were forced to work first on the plantations, and then as the labor force that laid track and dug tunnels for railroads, worked in prison factories and on state prison farms, mined coal, and built roads and canals, their capacity to sustain relations with family and community were seriously affected. The . . . [justification for]

their being "forced" into these labor roles was based on the popular notions that they were not only inferior but prone to criminality. . . . Consequently, the law, custom, and physical force were used to keep African Americans "in their place"—i.e., perpetual bondage. . . . An example of the songs that grew out of the practice of criminalizing African Americans is the following:

Standin' on de corner, weren't doin' no hahm, Up come a 'liceman an' he grab me by de ahm. Blow a little whistle an' ring a little bell; Heah come 'rol wagon a runnin' like hell.

Judge he call me up an' ast mah name, Ah told him fo' sho' Ah weren't to blame. He wink at 'liceman, 'liceman wink too; Judge he say, "Nigger, you get some work to do."

Workin' on ol' road bank, shackle boun', Long, long time fo' six months roll aroun'. Miserin' fo' my honey, she misern' fo' me, But, Lawd, white folks won't let go holdin' me.

Southern blacks were subjected to the demeaning practices of segregation, which included separate public drinking fountains like this one in Georgia.

tinue to oppress blacks and deprive them of many of their rights of citizenship, particularly the right to vote.

In addition to segregation, the threat of intimidation and violence in the form of lynching and white race riots grew worse between the 1890s and the 1910s. Continual harassment and violence was meted out by the white supremacist group the Ku Klux Klan (KKK), which was reestablished in 1919 after being disbanded decades earlier. The KKK grew into a massive national organization calling for Anglo-Saxon supremacy and terrorizing blacks with beatings, cross burnings, lynchings, and kidnappings. Historian Nell Painter notes,

The way white supremacists made sure that ex-slaves would fall back into place or nearly back into place [where they had been during slavery] was terror . . . beating people up, burning down their houses, shooting them—the mayhem of personal violence.[15]

It was out of this period of hardship and violence near the turn of the twentieth century that a new music began to come together. Out of the traditions of oral narrative and rhythms from Africa, out of the plaintive hollers, the agricultural, and chain gang songs, and the ballads, rose a sound unlike any before it. It was called the blues.

Chapter Two

Country Blues

Scholars believe that the first blues music developed in the rural Deep South in the last decade of the nineteenth century. Now called country blues or folk blues, this early version of the music was largely played by little-known musicians decades before the first blues recordings were made, so much is unknown about its earliest developments and players. However, by 1900, the blues existed in many places in the South and Midwest, and by this time the first known blues musicians were playing a variety of styles of the music.

The blues is an adaptable music, and it changed and modified as it spread from region to region and from player to player, via traveling musicians. As it moved through the country, the music picked up influences from other music and regional cultures, incorporated different instruments, had multiple playing techniques, and used a variety of song lyrics, often based on local stories or events. Therefore, "country blues" is a broad term that includes many different regional styles of acoustic (nonelectrified) rural blues that developed in the early twentieth century.

Regional Styles

Early country blues styles included Delta blues, Texas blues, and Piedmont blues, among others. These terms can be misleading because they can be used to denote either the region the music style came from or the musical style itself, and sometimes they are used to denote both. For instance, the Delta blues is often identified with the Mississippi Delta region in the southern part of the state of Mississippi, where the style is believed to have come from; however, the term is also often used to describe the style of music without regard to location, since many musicians who played it were not from or did not live in southern Mississippi.

Similarly, whereas the Piedmont region of the United States is a specific location near the Appalachian Mountains, the term "Piedmont blues" broadly encompasses the family of similar blues styles coming out of numerous states in the southeast, including Georgia, the Carolinas, Virginia, Florida, and West Virginia, as well as places as far north as Delaware and Massachusetts.

Thus, as most historians and musicologists use them, such terms describe musical styles that tend to be associated historically with certain regions but whose practitioners were not necessarily from or living in those areas.

The Birthplace of the Blues

The blues first developed in areas of the South where blacks worked the hardest and the labor was the most grueling: the Deep South and Texas. While some scholars disagree, many believe

Stavin' Chain performs a song in Lafayette, Louisiana, in 1934. Blues music began developing in the poorest regions of the Deep South.

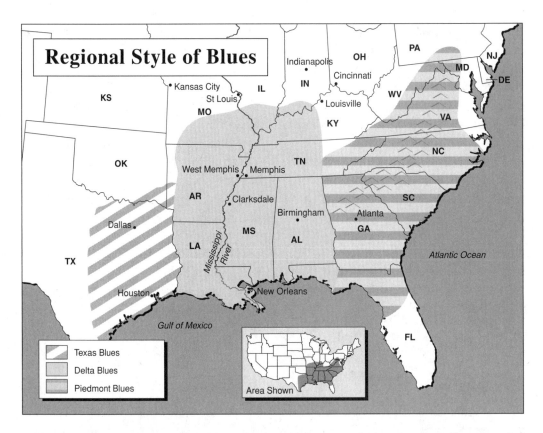

Regional Style of Blues

Texas Blues
Delta Blues
Piedmont Blues

Area Shown

the earliest blues came out of the Mississippi Delta. Richest in agriculture and white wealth, this region was also the poorest area of the country for blacks. Their lives were often very difficult and filled with hard labor, racist attitudes, and little financial reward.

The Mississippi Delta was frontier land for much of the nineteenth century. According to one traveler who saw the land before it was cleared, it was "jungle equal to any in Africa."[16] The soil was particularly rich due to deposits left by the Mississippi River, but until late in the century, it was unusable for farming because it was covered in forest and swamps, and was

subject to frequent flooding by the great waterway.

However, in 1870 the government began massive efforts to manage the river's flow along its entire twenty-three-hundred-mile course through the Midwest and South by building levees, dikes, and other constructions— an effort that continues to the present day. In his 1874 book *Life on the Mississippi,* author Mark Twain observed,

The military engineers . . . have taken upon their shoulders the job of making the Mississippi over again—a job transcended in size by only the original job of creating it.[17]

Once this effort was underway, settlers poured into the region, and many established vast cotton plantations there. These plantations required laborers to build levees along the river, to cut down the forests, to drain the swamps, and to do the hard work of farming the cotton. Plantation owners were prosperous, and to further maximize their profits, they hired massive amounts of cheap labor. During the time of slavery, such work had been performed by slaves, but in the postwar years plantation owners enticed free blacks to come work in the region by offering higher wages than elsewhere in the South, as well as other incentives. These incentives included free land for blacks to farm and supposedly better living and working conditions. As Lomax writes,

> Stories drifted back to the [East] that in the Delta greenbacks [dollars] grew on trees and the ponds were filled with molasses. There was plenty of work for axmen to clear forests and plenty of land for good farmers to raise cotton. The plantation owners needed hands and did everything they could to attract labor. [18]

Thousands of blacks went to the Delta, and by 1890 the region was more

This drawing shows a scene on the Mississippi River in the nineteenth century. By 1890 more African Americans lived in the Mississippi Delta than in any other region of the country.

densely populated with African Americans than any other in the country. For most, despite the abundance of work and the opportunity to sharecrop on their own land, life was hard. Many did backbreaking labor in the fields, forests, swamps, levees, and mud from dawn to dark for forty cents a day (about four dollars a day by today's standards). Many of the men were itinerant workers, living in dirty and violent work camps, separated from their families. Further, those who owned land were routinely cheated by landlords, often through elaborate schemes whereby farmers anticipating the proceeds from half their crop (the other half went to the landlord) would find that they had been charged high prices and interest on loans for food, tools, and other furnishings—many of which were never asked for or received.

Delta Blues

Thus, the delta was an apt birthplace for a music reflecting the hardships of black life. By the early twentieth century the Mississippi Delta had developed a distinct regional style of music called Delta blues, in which musicologists see close links to the early songs and shouts of laborers living in the region. Musician and historian Robert Palmer writes:

The simplest way to characterize the music's origin is as a turn-of-the-century innovation, accommodating the vocal traditions of work songs and field hollers to express capabilities of a newly popular stringed instrument, the guitar. Older black ballads and dance songs, preaching and church singing, the rhythms of folk drumming . . . fed into the new music as well. But the richly ornamented, powerfully projected singing style associated with the field hollers was dominant, which is hardly surprising; the Delta is more or less one big cotton field. [19]

The voice and guitar were the key instrumental components of most regional country blues styles and were particularly important to the Delta blues. Guitars were natural instruments for early blues players for several reasons: They were affordable, portable, and, perhaps most important, able to produce the so-called blue notes associated with the African vocal scale, which give the music its powerful emotional quality.

While traditional African or makeshift instruments had been common in black music for centuries, around the turn of the twentieth century harmonicas and guitars became the popular instruments of choice. Harmonicas—also called mouth harps—became widely available in the United States in the late nineteenth century. In the 1850s German instrument maker Matthias Hohner adapted the Chinese reed instrument known as the *cheng* into what is now known as the harmonica. The harmonica was portable and affordable, and became popular in America in the late nineteenth century. Around the same time, the Sears and Roebuck mail-order catalog began sell-

Delta Music

In his book The Bluesmen, *historian Samuel Charters explains that the Delta blues—considered by many to be the earliest form of the blues—had very little European influence. This was because African Americans in the Mississippi Delta were unusually isolated by the racist social system of the region.*

The music of the delta bears the marks of [the racial] separation between the people of the delta. Negroes were more heavily concentrated in the delta than they were in many other areas of the South, and because of the violence of the Mississippi caste system they were kept at an even further distance from the influence of southern white music. With the exception of a few small groups—the people of the sea islands of Georgia and the Carolinas and the families living in the Talladega Forest of Alabama who were so isolated that they retained even fragments of African speech—the delta field hands were less a part of southern life than any other large Negro group. The music that developed in the counties of the delta was so little influenced by American popular music that it was still closely related to the distant African background, and in many ways seemed to be an intense distillation of the slave music that had emerged from the diffuse tribal and cultural influences of the slave society.

ing acoustic guitars for between two and three dollars. These guitars, called Stellas, were purchased in great numbers. Almost everyone in the South had a Stella and almost all of the players were self-taught.

Delta Slide or "Bottleneck" Guitar

Whereas standard guitars were made of wood, in the early 1900s, louder-sounding aluminum-body guitars, known as Dobros or resonators, also became common in the Delta blues, particularly for those using the bottleneck, or slide, technique of playing, a variation that helped to define the Delta style. In this method of playing, in addition to or instead of depressing the strings with the fretting hand, the musician holds a piece of metal or glass against the strings. The object is often a knife edge or the end of a narrow-mouthed bottle worn on the end of a finger. (This is where the term "bottleneck guitar" comes from.) The sound made while the material slides up and down the strings is an emotive wailing sound that approximates the sound of a human voice.

The guitar, and particularly slide guitar, became a second voice for the blues singer to converse with. Many Delta blues musicians would sing a line and then make the guitar respond with its wail. Scholars believe this dialogue between player and instrument comes from the black church tradition of call-and-response, in which the preacher would cry out to the congregation and they would shout back their answer, as well as from the hollers shouted across the cotton fields.

Piedmont and Texas Styles

Each country blues style had its own distinct sound, influenced by instrument selection and playing techniques. For instance, the twelve-string guitar was often favored in the Piedmont style, which, as journalist Alan Coukell indicates, is one of the more mixed styles of blues, "reflect[ing] a mixing of cultures: African-American blues, white country picking, and English fiddle tunes." [20] This unique mix of influences created a style particularly noted for its quick and fancy finger work and highly syncopated playing, meaning the musician accents or stresses certain notes by playing them more strongly to give the music a rise-and-fall cadence. Further, the music was characterized by a strong alternating bass line, in which the musician picked alternate low strings with the thumb while a chorus of higher strings were

Huddie Ledbetter, known as Leadbelly, was one of the most influential blues artists associated with the Texas style.

plucked with the fingers. The music was lively and more upbeat than the Delta blues and was considered good party and dance music.

Texas blues encompassed a number of variations in instrument and technique. The Texas style was typically slower rhythmically than the Delta and Piedmont styles; however, two of the earliest and most influential musicians associated with Texas style were exceptions. Huddie Ledbetter, better known as Leadbelly, preferred the twelve-string guitar, and Blind Lemon Jefferson, considered one of the founders of Texas blues, was known for his own unique fast and intricate finger work, which he picked up in his youth from Mexican flamenco guitarists in Texas. These variations gave each musician his own distinct style, which others were eager to copy. The twelve-string guitar gave a fuller sound simply because there were more strings to make the sound, and Jefferson's quick, fancy fretting was picked up by many imitators.

The Beat and the Voice

No matter the variations in style, rhythm was of great importance to all blues. This defining quality of the music most likely came from rhythm's central importance in African musical traditions. Since black slaves in much of the South had been forbidden drums for centuries, these instruments were not present in most early country blues styles. Rather, blues musicians beat the ground with their feet to keep time and add rhythm. Some even slapped or knocked the wood of the guitar while they played.

The lyrics of the country blues came out of the fields and the black churches, as well as out of the traditions, experiences, and folklore known to the people who played it. As such, the lyrics were sung in the language and idiom of the poor black people from which they came. Further, while there were several common variations in the structure of early blues lyrics, they were most commonly simple, like the hollers and jump-ups from which they were derived.

Like playing styles, blues songs and lyrics passed from one player to the next as musicians shared their music with each other. Unlike in contemporary times, when copying another person's songs or lyrics is considered stealing, there was no such concept in early blues songwriting. Rather, as journalist Richard Newman writes, the music was passed along as in the African oral tradition:

> Early African American music was completely democratic. There were no titles, dates, or names of lyricists or composers. Nor was anything written down. The music came from the people, and those who created this living tradition preserved it, sustained it, and passed it on to their descendants. [21]

The lyrics of blues songs prior to the World War II era were generally taken from a floating pool of lines and verses. For example, lines or phrases such as "I can't be satisfied" and "Laughing to keep from crying" appeared in dozens of songs.

Commonly, one musician would learn a song from another and then adapt it. He or she might keep the lyrics or change them, shuffle them, or completely rewrite them to suit his or her needs. Even the same player would often change the lyrics to suit his or her audience, circumstance, or mood.

Form of the Blues

As a folk art—learned, played, and adapted informally rather than through instruction or use of sheet music—the blues was diverse, with songs taking many different structures. However, the most common blues form is the twelve-bar structure, played in 4/4 time. This means that each song has twelve musical measures with four beats per measure, and each quarter note is equal to one beat.

The twelve-bar blues was divided into three sections, with four bars in each. These sections corresponded to three lines of lyrics, which is the most common arrangement in a blues stanza. Most blues songs follow one of two patterns: AAA or AAB. Many early blues songs were AAA, containing three-line stanzas with a single verse repeated three times. For example:

I'm a po' boy 'long way from home,
I'm a po' boy 'long way from home,
Oh, I'm a po' boy 'long way from home. [22]

The AAB variation became the most common form. It was also based on a three-line stanza, but the first line was sung twice and a second, different line was sung once. Often the first line set up a question or a situation that the third line answered or resolved. For example:

Ev'ry day, seems like murder here,
Ev'ry day, seems like murder here,

I'm gonna leave tomorrow, I know you don't want me here. [23]

Themes and Subjects

The lyrics of the blues were also often personal expressions of a player's feelings or situation. This is the most fundamental difference between blues lyrics and those of earlier black music such as ragtime or ballads. Whether the songs were made up by the musician or by someone else, they expressed individual feelings and emotional involvement. Palmer writes,

> Those earlier songs about possums and train engineers and desperadoes deal in archetypes [models]. The singer remains relatively cool and uninvolved. In the blues, there is no narration as such, and while one finds signs and symbols and proverbial homilies aplenty there is nothing as abstract as an archetype. The singer is so involved that in many cases his involvement becomes both the subject and substance of the work. [24]

The country blues, like all blues, dealt with a variety of emotional themes—loneliness, hardship, partings, rambling, and other aspects of black life. The rambling life of a musician, for instance, was filled with both the excitement and loneliness of moving around. Lomax says, "[Blues] was a music suited to the life of wandering people. It spoke

Secret Expression

Black sharecroppers and tenant farmers of the South struggled to survive in a corrupt system that often kept them poor and unable to improve their conditions. As Paul Oliver explains in his book Blues Fell Like Rain, *some of the earliest blues was born out of this plight as song became the only safe place to secretly express sorrow, anger, and frustration. As an example, he uses a song by an unknown blues musician.*

Both share-cropper and tenant-farmer had to "stay in good" with their White overlords and . . . no Negro dared raise his voice aloud in protest or assert his rights when he was the victim of racial discrimination. So he maintained an air of happy indolence, played up to the stereotypes that traditional jokes had moulded for him, hid his sufferings and struggled to survive.

Well, I drink to keep from worrying and I laugh to keep from crying, (twice) I keep a smile on my face so the public won't know my mind.

Some people thinks I am happy but they sho' don't know my mind, (twice) They see this smile on my face, but my heart is bleeding all the time.

A family of black tenant farmers works the cotton fields outside their run-down living quarters on an Alabama plantation.

of partings, of oppression, and . . . homelessness." [25]

However, the blues was not depressing music; despite the fact that it sung of hardships, it did so with a certain understanding and humor. Lomax continues:

> The tales and songs return again and again to a few themes—to the grievous and laughable ironies in the lives of an outcaste people, who were unfairly denied the rewards of an economy they had helped to build. One black response to this ironic fact was to create the blues—the first satirical song form in the English language. [26]

The blues also served to allow blacks a voice with which to express their feelings about their lives in the safe space of a song. Like the old spirituals, work songs, and field hollers that dominated during slavery, the blues, rising as it did out of a time of racial oppression and segregation, often contained meanings that were hidden from whites. For example, some-

The lyrics of the blues reflected the hardships that tenant farmers and sharecroppers like this Mississippi man faced in their daily lives.

times a blues musician would sing about how bad and mean his woman was to him, when in fact he was actually talking about his landlord or boss. Whites tended to ignore or not understand the undercurrents of such music, but it was a means of catharsis for many mistreated blacks.

Other subjects the blues dealt with were local hardships and disasters. These included the great boll weevil infestation that destroyed cotton crops in the mid-1910s and contributed to the beginning of the Great Migration of many Southern blacks to northern industrial cities, and the 1927 Mississippi River flood—the largest hydrological event of the twentieth century—which submerged much of the delta. However, as historian Giles Oakley writes, more personal themes, particularly the theme of sexual relationships between men and women, dominated the blues:

> The principal theme of the country blues, and probably of all blues, is the sexual relationship. Almost all other themes, leaving town, train rides, work trouble, general dissatisfaction sooner or later reverts to the central concern. Most frequently the core of the relationship is seen as inherently unstable, transient, but with infinite scope for pleasure and exultation in success, or pain and torment in failure. This gives the blues its tension and ambiguity, dealing simultaneously with togetherness and loneliness, communion and isolation, physical joy and emotional anguish. [27]

Life of a Bluesman
The themes, words, and music of the blues grew out of the lives of the people who played them. While many of the early blues players were themselves laborers, who, as one of them said, would "plow a mule in daytime, pick a guitar at night," [28] many of the earliest known blues musicians were also wanderers. While some worked as itinerant laborers, some blues players avoided or left hard labor for music and scrambled constantly to get enough money to keep themselves going. They moved from place to place, playing at work camps, picnics, train stations, white honky tonks, brothels, and often on the street. Most were loners without homes, and many were frequently hard-drinking womanizers. Many died violent deaths.

The First Known Bluesman
The first blues musician whose name and music is still known was a good example of such hard and fast living. He was a delta musician named Charley Patton, considered by many to be not only the first but among the greatest and most influential of all the early country blues musicians.

Born in 1887 on a farm near Edwards, Mississippi, Patton moved with his family to the Dockery Plantation, a vast cotton center in the heart of the delta near Tutwiler and Sumner, around 1897. Patton worked on the plantation

Voodoo at the Crossroads

In addition to musical traditions, among the cultural practices Africans brought with them to America was voodoo, an African animist religion that survived alongside Christianity in many slave cultures and whose traditions, folklore, and figures became important to the blues. Among the most prominent voodoo gods to be featured in blues folklore was Legba, Master of the Crossroads, a feared yet beloved trickster who plays mischief on deities and human beings. Many scholars say that Legba is the voodoo antecedent of the devil as he figures in much blues lore, particularly in the stories of blues guitarists such as Tommy Johnson and Robert Johnson selling their souls at the crossroads to achieve their musical talent. In the following excerpt, taken from Julio Finn's book The Bluesman, *Tommy Johnson's brother Ledell describes how his brother struck his deal with Legba/the Devil.*

Now, if Tom was living, he'd tell you. He said the reason he knowed so much [music], said he sold hisself to the devil. I asked him how. He said, "If you want to learn how to play anything you want to play and learn how to make songs yourself, you take your guitar and you go to where the road crosses that way, where a crossroads is. Get there, be sure to get there just a little 'fore 12:00 that night. . . . You have your guitar and be playing a piece there by yourself. . . . A big black man will walk up there and take your guitar, and he'll tune it. And then he'll play a piece and then hand it back to you. That's the way I learned to play anything I want."

Blues musicians Tommy Johnson and Robert Johnson claimed they sold their souls to the devil himself.

as a field hand and a wagon driver while learning how to play the guitar from other musicians who lived there. Because of the number of blues musicians who lived and played on the plantation, by 1900 Dockery had become famous throughout the delta as a place to learn the blues.

After learning to play, Patton left the plantation frequently, roaming and playing at other plantations or homes for his dinner or playing at roadhouses, dance halls, and house parties. He played in traveling medicine shows and drifted to various other delta towns, playing with other musicians such as Texan Blind Lemon Jefferson, who would become one of the first recorded blues stars, and Willie Brown. Like many musicians of his time, Patton played the blues for himself and for black audiences, but he also played country, ragtime, and other popular music—anything to please an audience of either color. Historian Samuel Charters writes,

> He sang for everybody in the delta, white and colored, and he had songs for every kind of audience. Nearly half of the songs that he recorded were play party songs or folk songs, country ballads or gospel songs. . . . His blues were among the most compelling and individual of the early blues period. [29]

Patton became known as a musical clown and an entertainer because he

Charley Patton is recognized as the first and one of the greatest country blues musicians.

would do tricks with his guitar, such as playing the guitar behind his back or throwing it into the air and catching it between his legs, all while continuing to play a song.

Patton also gained a reputation as a hard drinker and womanizer, having two wives and a longtime mistress, with whom he lived for several years. He was frequently arrested, and he knew almost every lawman in the delta and even featured some of them in his songs. One particularly harsh sheriff was immortalized in Patton's song "High Sheriff Blues":

> Let me tell you folkses, how he treated me, umhuh, Let me tell you folkses, how he treated me, umhuh, And he put me in the cellar just as dark as it could be. [30]

Additionally, he slurred, shortened, or ran words into each other to suit the rhythm of his playing to the point that they were impossible to understand. As his fellow bluesman and student Son House said, "A lot of Charley's words . . . you can be sitting right under him . . . you can't hardly understand him." [31]

But it was Patton's blues style rather than his lyrics that was most influential to many other delta musicians. His slide guitar playing and his voice, which could be rough and raw one moment and soft and sweet another, were his trademarks. He taught or directly influenced many of the other great blues guitarists of his generation and those that followed, including Son House, Skip James, Howlin' Wolf, Robert Johnson, and Muddy Waters.

Despite their local popularity, men like Patton and the country blues artists he influenced were mostly unknown until their first recordings were made. Although the styles of country blues that developed early in the twentieth century were likely the oldest and most deeply influential forms of the music, it would not be until the mid-1920s that they would first become widely heard, and even then, only because of the success of more sophisticated blues that had been adapted for city life.

Chapter Three

Popularization of the Blues

The 1920s and 1930s was a period of great popularization of the blues. Along with migrating black workers and traveling musicians, strains of country blues moved into the cities, where its lyrics, styles, and themes were adapted to suit the new environment.

The early music that grew out of this adaptation was called city blues and was the first of the blues to be recorded and commercially marketed. When city blues music became instantly popular and profitable, country blues was also recorded for the first time, allowing country bluesmen like Charley Patton, Blind Lemon Jefferson, and others to have their music disseminated, changing the flavor and history of the blues forever.

Through the use of new instruments, lyrics, and playing styles, city blues styles became established in many cities throughout the South, Midwest, and Northeast, including Chicago, Louisville, Indianapolis, Cleveland, Cincinnati, St. Louis, New York, Kansas City, and New Orleans. A few cities, such as St. Louis, New Orleans, and New York, were particularly significant sites for the development of early city blues.

"Father of the Blues"

Although cities became significant sites for the blues, the first well-noted discovery of the blues occurred not in an urban environment but in rural Mississippi, by a man who would first bring the music—at least his interpretation of the music—to a wider audience. In 1903 a popular southern black band leader and music publisher named William Christopher "W.C." Handy, who had recently moved to Mississippi, was waiting for a long-delayed train in a station in the town of Tutwiler, not far from Dockery Farms, where Charley Patton and many other great blues guitarists learned to play. As he waited, he heard a poor black man playing what was to him a strange kind of music on the guitar. The man used a knife blade on the strings as a slide and repeated a single, mournful lyric again and again as he did: "Goin' where the Southern cross the Dog,"[32] he sang. (Handy later found out that "the Southern" and "the Dog" were nicknames for the two major railroads in the area and the man was singing about the place where they crossed paths—the place where the man was going to take the train.)

Handy listened, enthralled by this music, which he later described as the weirdest he had ever heard. It was, of course, the Delta blues, and over the next several years, Handy heard and paid attention to more rural blues around him. Using key elements from the music— its rhythms and lyrics—he wrote and published sheet music for several blues songs.

Handy's songs were much closer to popular ragtime pieces than to the rural blues from which he had borrowed. However, his songs, such as "Memphis Blues" and "St. Louis Blues," were big hits. Other ragtime composers such as Scott Joplin picked up on this new music. It was played, written, and listened to by blacks and whites alike and became extremely popular in the mid-1910s, leading to what some describe as a "blues craze." Because of Handy's role in first spreading this adapted form of the blues, he became known as the Father of the Blues.

Vaudeville Entertainers

However, despite Handy's popularity as the self-proclaimed discoverer of the blues, as Palmer writes, it was traveling stage musicians that first picked up on country blues and brought it to the cities in an adapted form: "The first blues heard outside the rural South was performed and disseminated by black vaudeville entertainers . . . who stumbled on the music in the course of their travels."[33]

Vaudeville, then, was the means by which the blues first entered American popular culture. Vaudeville had become a significant form of popular entertainment following the Civil War and had grown steadily in importance into the early decades of the twentieth century as new vaudeville theaters sprang up in many cities following World War I. According to scholars at the University of Virginia,

The development of vaudeville marked the beginning of popular entertainment as big business, dependent on the organizational efforts of a growing number of white-collar workers and the increased leisure time, spending power, and changing tastes of an urban middle class audience.[34]

Vaudeville shows were variety entertainment, often including comedy, dance, and music. The headline events of the shows were musical acts, most frequently led by a black female singer, often accompanied variously by horn players, pianists, and guitars. Some of the singers even led their own bands, but the black female leads were the biggest draw for audiences. As one critic said,

*W.C. Handy makes musical notations as he composes the song "St. Louis Blues,"
one of his big blues hits.*

"No road show was complete without a
[black] momma singing the blues."[35]

In the South, touring vaudeville
groups heard the blues and began in-
corporating songs and aspects of the music into their own repertoire, with the influences of jazz and ragtime mixed in.
One of the most influential early blues
singers, Gertrude "Ma" Rainey, claimed
to have heard the blues in a small rural
town as early as 1902 in southern Mis-
souri, where she was performing in a

traveling tent show. She recalled, "A girl
from the town . . . came to the tent one
morning and began to sing about the
'man' who had left her. . . ."[36]

Rainey liked the touching song and
adapted it into her own act. Music historians believe that these borrowings
from rural blues made a major contri-
bution to spreading the blues throughout the South.

Further, singers like Rainey carried
this music north, where it became

popular entertainment. Similar to the Delta country blues tradition, the blues these female entertainers sang was marked by powerful, often rough vocalization.

Classic Female Blues

Many of the best female vaudeville singers whose popularity was based on their blues-influenced music eventually worked their way into nightclubs in cities such as Chicago and New York City's Harlem. Among these performers were Ida Cox, Ma Rainey, Mamie Smith, and Bessie Smith (no relation).

Bessie Smith is considered the queen of the classic female blues style.

In many cities during the 1920s, jazz music gained great popularity and many of these performers came to be identified as part of the Jazz Age. While their songs were different from the rural country blues and the music had been influenced by jazz, the blues influence particularly showed through in their lyrics, which were usually about trouble, love, and loss. Like all blues, the lyrics were often filled with irony, sexual innuendo, and humor.

This style of blues later became known as classic female blues, an early city style that one critic called "a wedding of southern folk cosmology and the jazzlike accompaniment of a piano or small ensemble."[37] Because of the successful sales of the first blues recordings in the 1920s, this style would have a greater impact on the popularization of the blues than W.C. Handy's early sheet music compositions.

Early City Blues Styles

Scholars believe that many city blues styles developed at almost the same time as country blues was evolving. Others see more of a direct evolution from country to city styles. Regardless of which school of thought is correct, it is certain that the blues developed in several cities quite early and it is certain that the rural and city music shared a common lineage.

City styles were distinctive from country styles, yet, as scholar Jon Michael Spencer notes, city and country styles also shared certain qualities:

Ma Rainey and her Georgia Jazz Band perform in Chicago in 1923. Rainey began her famed career as a vaudeville performer.

City blues of the 1920s and beyond was essentially an urbanized or "citified" country blues. . . . City blues became an intensified country sound. It was also country in that it was fundamentally a verbal, or spoken, genre (revealing its kinship with hollers).[38]

Instruments of City Blues

The sound of the city blues also differed in the breadth and type of instruments played by the musicians. Whereas the country styles usually included an acoustic guitar played alone or accompanied by a harmonica, city blues often incorporated the piano and a new invention called the electric guitar.

The first electric guitar was introduced in 1933 by a company called Vivi-Tone and was quickly taken up by blues musicians. The sound of the electric guitar was louder than the acoustic and could sustain notes for longer periods of time. The intensity of the sound matched the more lively and loud environment of the city.

The piano was no stranger in the country. Many country blues musicians played in camps and taverns along the Mississippi, including the rough and rowdy taverns of lumber camps known as barrelhouses (where barrels of liquor were kept). This barrelhouse piano sound became a popular early blues style characterized by its loud, percussive playing. Its sound was booming and rhythmic, with the musician's left hand banging out a walking bass line while the right created the melody.

However, many piano players found that they could make a better living in the cities, so while the piano is not exclusive to the city style, the cities were where piano blues tended to evolve.

St. Louis Blues

The piano was particularly important to the development of the blues in cities such as East St. Louis, Illinois. At the time, the blues was thought of by most people as music for poor blacks, and, indeed, blues was popular in the predominantly black-populated city. The blues could be heard all over the city, in its lurid red light district night clubs, gambling houses, and brothels, as well as at the so-called rent parties, where people who were short on their rent threw live-music events to make up the extra cash. The blues could also be heard at sporting centers, which were often filled with opportunists and criminals, as well as the poor, gamblers, revelers, and blues musicians.

This music—called St. Louis blues—was usually a group endeavor, with bands made up of singers, a piano, and a few other instruments, primarily for rhythm. In St. Louis and other city blues towns, particularly popular was the blues sound known as boogie-woogie, which could be played on a guitar but was most suited for the piano. A fast-paced and rhythmic method of playing, boogie-woogie had evolved from musicians using their instruments to mimic the sound of a steam engine running

down the tracks. The name boogie-woogie matched the rhythmic, swinging sound of the beat. On the piano, the left hand played a repetitive rhythmic and melodic pattern in the bass keys while the right hand played improvised variations of the melody in the treble keys. This significant sound remained popular in the blues and the music it influenced, including later urban styles like jump blues and the rhythm and blues of the 1940s and 1950s, as well as rock and roll.

New Orleans

Historically, New Orleans is best known for its jazz; however, it had an active and early blues culture. Jelly Roll Morton, who was one of the best-known ragtime and jazz composers and pianists, recalled hearing the blues in New Orleans in 1902, a year before Handy's famous discovery of rural blues in Tutwiler. Morton recalled, "Music was pouring into the streets from every house. Women were standing in the doorways, singing or chanting some kind of blues—some very happy, some very sad." [39]

New Orleans blues was unique in that it used horns and drums, which had never been forbidden to black musicians during slavery; thus, by the twentieth century, along with the piano, these instruments dominated both jazz and the blues. Music historian Cub Koda describes the styles as "enlivened by Caribbean rhythms, an unrelenting party atmosphere and the . . . strut of the Dixieland music so indigenous to the area . . . [with] vocals

Blues and Gospel

The blues, unlike its cousin, gospel, which had grown out of the tradition of spirituals and the Christianization of African Americans, was a secular music. However, although the division between spiritual music and secular music was distinct, many blues musicians were also active in the church. Many of the same hard-drinking, womanizing bluesmen who stayed up all Saturday night playing the blues were the same people who were lay preachers and played or sang along to gospel music the next morning in church. As Harley Cokliss notes in his film Chicago Blues, *the blues and gospel shared many traits.*

Blues and gospel speak the same language. The storefront church belongs to the same world as the tavern and nightclub. There is the same sense of community. The same knowledge that the brother singing or talking up there knows what you feel. But the blues is about the troubles of this world. It doesn't offer solutions. It's a lament. Gospel has a solution: God is the answer.

Gospel singers liven up the stage at the New Orleans Jazz Festival in 1991. Blues and gospel are very close musical cousins.

[running] the emotional gamut from laid-back crooning to full-throated Gospel shouting."[40]

The Dixieland influence and the horns of New Orleans blues gave it a brassier sound. Additionally, the beat was often slightly out of step with the melody, as if the rhythm section was trying to catch up with the melody of the horns. This element gave New Or-

Recording the Blues

As Bruce Eder describes in his "Beginner's Guide and History—How to Listen to the Blues," in the All Music Guide to the Blues, *when the blues recordings were made in the 1920s and 1930s, the recording process, financial arrangements, and distribution were informal by contemporary standards.*

Recording was a haphazard process—microphones were crude, the fidelity sometimes doubtful, and recording tape didn't exist. The recording process in those days involved cutting a hot wax lacquer at 78 rpm, on a portable machine (that might weigh hundreds of pounds). There was no such thing as "playback," which would ruin the lacquer—recording couldn't be checked for errors until a pressing was prepared, as much as a month later, so it was up to the musician and the producer, faced with limited time and money, to recognize whether a song was captured at its best. . . .

According to the recollections of some participants, the fees, such as they were could be as little as $50 to $100 and a supply of gin or bourbon for an afternoon's recording session that might yield four to six songs. Royalties, even when they were part of the contract, which would have been extraordinary, seem seldom to have been paid, and even if a musician were interested in formally copyrighting an original song, there was no way in those days to collect royalties on its sales. . . .

The business of selling records was very different then. Record stores existed, but they were really music stores that carried sheet music and even piano rolls in the early days as well as 78-rpm platters. Records were less important than sheet music and most of what the biggest stores stocked was classical music and . . . popular music, and jazz. If the blues were carried at all, it was only in the stores in neighborhoods—such as New York's Harlem and Chicago's South Side—that had large enough numbers of customers for them.

leans blues its swinging, slightly disjointed sound.

Harlem

Of all the many cities where the blues made its mark during the early decades of the twentieth century, few music scenes were as well known as the one in the predominantly black Manhattan neighborhood of Harlem. Harlem gained great fame during the 1920s and 1930s as the home of a burgeoning African American literary, musical, and cultural movement known as the Harlem Renaissance. It was also considered the center of the Jazz Age of the 1920s, which was heavily influenced by the blues brought to it by vaudeville singers such as Ma Rainey and Bessie Smith.

During the Harlem Renaissance's heyday, the neighborhood was crowded with jazz and blues musicians playing everywhere from high-priced nightclubs such as the Cotton Club, where jazz dominated, to the rent parties, speakeasies, and other places where blues was the music of choice. Additionally, Harlem Renaissance writers such as Langston Hughes celebrated the blues of the time in his writing, creating one of his most famous poems, "The Weary Blues," about a blues musician at a piano.

Out of this musical scene, the most famous of the classic female blues artists rose to stardom and the first blues recordings were made, an event that would launch a new era of popular music as well as the black music recording industry.

Race Records

By the time the first blues phonograph record was pressed in 1920, the technology to make phonograph records was twenty-three years old. However, until the first blues record came out, blacks had not been a significant market for records. Recordings of blacks singing formal arrangements of spirituals and other songs had become popular with whites and some middle-class blacks around 1900. Similar audiences also listened to jazz recordings, with whites playing music originally developed by black jazz musicians.

However, record companies recognized that with a large population of nearly 14 million blacks in the country, few of whom were buying records, they were missing a large potential market. With that in mind, companies decided to record the blues, which was most popular in places like Harlem with working-class and poor blacks. The first recording label to do so was a New York company called OKeh. In 1920, OKeh recorded Mamie Smith's "Crazy Blues," the first phonograph record to introduce the term "blues" to the popular music culture. Like Handy's compositions, the song was more ragtime vaudeville than blues, but it was closer to the blues than anything else recorded before it. It was also more popular than anyone expected. "Crazy Blues" sold seventy-five thousand copies a month, which was an astounding success for even very popular music in those days.

OKeh's success prompted many other companies to follow their example and begin recording female blues singers. Soon, several companies were promoting the recordings of Ma Rainey, Alberta Hunter, and Bessie Smith, the last considered by most critics to be the queen of the classic female blues style. These records established a genre called "race recording" or "race music," which was the euphemistic way for companies to designate music marketed to black listeners.

Talent Searches

Record companies explored other variations of race recordings, including male singers and guitarists. Many of the musicians who had accompanied the female blues singers, including Louis Armstrong, went on to record alone or with their own bands. Some of them were from the South, such as Blind Lemon Jefferson, who was among the first country blues artists to record and become famous. According to music historian David Evans, although Jefferson was not the first blues musician, he was "generally—and appropriately—viewed by music historians as the first 'star' of this type of blues."[41] After he recorded his first sessions in 1926, the popularity of his records exceeded even those of Mamie Smith's, selling so many recordings that the wax masters from which copies of records were made wore out before the demand for his music did.

The success of the race-recording industry stimulated a search for new black talent, including rural singers and guitarists. Almost all of the recording

companies were located in Memphis, Chicago, and New York, which limited the pool of talent to those who lived in those cities or those who came with hopes of recording. To expand their search, record companies sent scouts—usually whites—into the South to find talent. The recording search was often like that of a local talent show. The agent would come into town and hold open auditions, often in a hotel lobby or in the local general store. Local musicians would come in, play a song or two, and if the scout liked what he heard, he signed the musician to a contract right then. However, only rarely did recordings take place in rural areas such as the Mississippi Delta. Blues musicians such as Charley Patton, Son House, and Skip James signed contracts and made arrangements to go to cities in the North to record. After they were finished they returned home to continue playing at their country venues.

Business Arrangements

Among the reasons recording labels scoured the South for new talent was that they could pay the musicians much less than they could the popular classic female blues singers who were able to command large fees for their talent. Although there were exceptions to the rule, most of the country blues players who were recorded never got rich from their recordings and few received the extensive fame Blind Lemon Jefferson experienced. Further, the onset of the Great Depression following the U.S. stock market crash in 1929 drove some

This is an autographed photo of Blind Lemon Jefferson, the first star of the Texas blues style.

recording companies out of business. One such label was Paramount Records, which had recorded numerous country blues guitarists. In some cases, recordings were not even released or were released in extremely limited runs.

However, because musicians like Charley Patton, Blind Lemon Jefferson, Son House, and other country blues artists were recorded, for the first time their music could be heard by a wider audience. Many critics say that many of

Folk Archival Recordings

As blues historian Richie Unterberger writes in "The Blues as Folklore" in the All Music Guide to the Blues, *folk archivist recordings made in the 1930s and 1940s were important to the development of the blues.*

[O]ur knowledge of traditional blues as a whole would be much poorer if not for the pioneering efforts of a few dedicated folklorists. . . .

By far the most important of these archivists were John A. Lomax and his son Alan. [In the early 1930s] the senior Lomax . . . was struggling to make a living at his chosen profession. [Lomax] became curator of the Library of Congress' Archive of Folk Song [which had a mission] of recording and preserving important American folk music. In these endeavors, he was greatly aided by his son Alan, who was still a teenager when the Lomaxes went on the road to collect songs . . . in 1933. . . .

The Lomaxes had only been on the road for a little over a month when they hit more paydirt than they could have expected. They did some of their recordings in prison, figuring that the long-time inmates were more apt to preserve traditional styles in the absence of contact from the outside world. July 1933 found them at Louisiana's Angola Penitentiary, where they discovered 12-string guitarist and singer Leadbelly, one of the major figures in 20th century American music. . . .

John and Alan Lomax didn't record only blues, or even focus on the blues . . . [but] Alan undertook his most important blues sessions on behalf of the Library of Congress in the early '40s, as part of a project documenting music in Coahoma County, MS. On these trips he found Muddy Waters and Son House, whose recordings were summaries of Delta blues styles past and present.

Alan Lomax (foreground) documents recordings of folk songs in the Library of Congress in this 1941 photo.

the country styles would most likely have died out or never had the influence that they did without these recordings. Further, blues guitarists were able to learn new songs, techniques, and styles of playing of other musicians without ever having met them.

A New Generation of Bluesmen

The phonograph record had a great impact on the history of the blues. Not only that, it affected blues styles. Up until the 1960s, most blues releases—indeed, most music in general—were produced as singles, with one song on each side of a lacquer disk. Often called 78s because they were played at seventy-eight revolutions per minute (rpm) on record players, these disks could hold songs approximately three minutes long. This was much shorter than most blues songs, which were often lengthy and could be extended with variations and improvisations by the musician for as long as he or she felt like playing. Thus, it was difficult for many blues musicians to alter their songs to fit phonograph records.

An important exception to this rule was Robert Johnson. Now a legendary figure in the blues, Johnson was a Delta blues guitar player who had learned from and played with many of the earliest great guitarists such as Charley Patton and Son House. Like blues guitarist Tommy Johnson before him, Robert Johnson claimed to have sold his soul to the devil at a Mississippi crossroads to learn how to play the guitar; however, Johnson in fact learned from a few good

teachers, practice, and a great deal from listening to 78s of other players.

By the mid 1930s the Great Depression had hit the blues recording industry fairly hard and few rural blues artists were being recorded any more. However, in 1936 and 1937, Johnson recorded two sessions, resulting in twenty songs, all of which he had polished and tailored to fit on 78s.

Like many country bluesmen, Johnson was a hard drinker and a womanizer, and in 1938, shortly after making his historic recordings, he was poisoned, either by a woman he had made advances toward or by her jealous husband. He died a few days later at home, at the age of twenty-seven. Johnson's haunting, crooning voice and masterly slide guitar made him one of the most admired blues musicians. Many critics attest that Johnson's recordings were a landmark in the evolution and popularization of the blues. He served as a bridge between the older country blues, which was steeped in the oral tradition, and the blues to come in the decades ahead, where recordings were more important than live performances to the survival and growth of the music. Writer and critic Russell Banks writes, "Johnson stood, then, at a crossroads: between the oral tradition and that of the phonograph record." [42]

By the late 1930s, the blues was a music in the throes of great transition. Popularized in its first decades through sheet music and then recording, it had evolved into numerous styles of the country and the city. However, its period of greatest influence and popularity was yet to come.

Chapter Four

Urban Blues

During the 1940s and 1950s, the blues reached its greatest popularity and widest influence up to that time. The first live blues-oriented radio programs began, many blues musicians toured the country to large, yet still predominantly black, audiences, and after the lull of the Depression, record companies produced more blues records.

In this boom time, the blues went through some significant changes in its styles and its instrumentation. As the Great Migration that began in the early twentieth century reached its peak during this period, the blues gained more popularity than ever in urban areas. New, sophisticated urban blues styles developed out of this trend, including the jazz-influenced jump blues and rhythm and blues (R&B).

While these genres emphasized the piano and horns over the guitar, urban blues, a guitar-dominated style drawn from transplanted and adapted Delta country blues traditions, arose during

the same period. Musicians had been using the electric guitar since the early 1930s, but it was the new urban style that relied most heavily on the instrument. Additionally, urban blues incorporated a new ensemble format of guitar, bass, drums, and harmonica. Pioneered by musicians like Delta-born Muddy Waters in Chicago, the urban blues became the foundation for some of the most prevalent and popular blues heard in later decades.

In addition to shifts in its styles, the blues found a new audience during these years. Like the blues styles before them, the new forms of the 1940s and 1950s were at first played by and for predominantly black audiences; however, during this period young, white audiences began listening to the new sounds of blues, particularly R&B. While black music had significantly influenced white music for a century or more, the blues and its artists made their significant and lasting impact on mainstream culture during this period when young, white musicians such as Elvis Presley and Jerry Lee Lewis adapted blues into a new, predominantly white form of popular music called rock and roll.

Changing with the Times

The changes that the blues went through during the 1940s and 1950s were part of a larger national cultural change brought on by World War II and postwar innovations and conditions. Among the most historically important technical innovations for the blues that were popularized during this era were the jukebox and the electric guitar.

The first phonograph jukeboxes were developed in the 1920s—some by companies that had formerly made

Elvis Presley, who grew up in the South listening to black urban blues, incorporated the blues into the new rock and roll music style.

automated player pianos—and they came into commercial use during the 1930s. By the 1940s, when technical improvements had made them more popular, they found their way into clubs, roadhouses, and bars, where they often replaced or supplemented live entertainment. These popular establishments, which became known as juke joints, sprang up all over the country, particularly in the South. For many people there, it was not affordable or convenient to purchase phonographs—there was no such thing as a record store yet—and jukeboxes were often the first and only source for new music, especially hard-to-find blues songs. As Lomax writes, jukeboxes were extremely important in the blues heartland of the Mississippi Delta:

I am not exaggerating when I say that this neon-lit, chrome-plated musical monster was for the people of the Delta not only their chief source of new songs but also an important symbol of democracy. . . . They put their money on the records they liked, and the rest went unplayed. [43]

Blues Goes Electric

However important the jukebox became, live performances of blues remained popular. In fact, many performances oc-

Farm workers dance in a juke joint in New Jersey in 1942. Jukeboxes offered affordable entertainment and helped to spread the popularity of blues music.

King Biscuit Time

During the early 1940s, KFFA in Helena, Arkansas, was the only radio station in the country that would play the blues—or any music by African Americans. The broadcast reached listeners throughout the Mississippi Delta region, and its blues program, *King Biscuit Time*, became extremely influential, inspiring later great blues musicians such as Riley "B.B." King, Ike Turner, Robert Nighthawk, and others, many of whom tuned in to the program during lunch breaks during their day jobs.

The popularity of the show also turned Helena into an even more influential blues center. The city became a hub for many blues musicians as they traveled from Memphis and the Delta into the North and back. When musicians were in Helena, they knew they could play with and hear some of the best musicians in the region.

Still broadcasting today, *King Biscuit Time* went on to become one of the longest running and most influential blues radio programs, being broadcast more times than popular programs such as *American Bandstand* and the *Grand Ole Opry*. Because it reached so wide an audience, the program was a major breakthrough for the blues and African American music in general, just as race records had been in the 1920s.

---

curred in juke joints, with the box filling in only when live musicians were absent.

Juke joints and other places where blues were played tended to be rowdy, crowded places, often with people gambling and making noise. It was for this reason that the electric guitar first became prevalent. Although they were first introduced in the early 1930s, it was not until the 1940s that electric guitars became widely used. Musicians needed to be heard over the crowd, so they amplified the instruments and their voices through microphones and loudspeakers.

In addition to the practical nature of the innovation, many blues and jazz guitarists enjoyed the new sounds and techniques made possible by the addition of electricity, and the instrument became popular for this reason as much as for its functional necessity. For example, on an electric guitar musicians could hold long, loud, wailing notes much longer than on an acoustic. Additionally, distortion could be added to give the notes a growling quality. Because of this, many critics and scholars mark the addition of electricity to the guitar as among the most important developments in the blues.

Radio

Another extremely important technical development was the increased use and prevalence of the radio. The radio first became popular as an entertainment medium during the late 1920s and 1930s. In fact, the accessibility of free music over the radio during the 1930s had contributed to the decline in the popularity and production of phonographs. It was not until the 1940s, however, that the blues was broadcast over the radio. During the 1940s and 1950s, the electrified blues reached its height of popularity through this medium.

In 1941 a businessman named Sam Anderson established a new radio station, KFFA, in the predominantly black east Arkansas city of Helena. Although a small city, Helena had such a strong blues tradition that many in the 1940s considered it a little Chicago. Helena was for many years an open town (meaning there was lax enforcement of the law) and had had its share of illegal industry, including bootlegging (illegal distribution and sale of liquor), supported by police corruption. As in many open towns along the Mississippi River, areas in which such illicit activity was prevalent also drew blues musicians who played in the clubs and bars.

When Anderson announced plans for the new radio station, the news spread quickly and two blues musicians living in Helena at the time—Sonny Boy Williamson II and Willie Miller—decided to see if they could get jobs playing live blues over the radio. When they auditioned for Anderson, he liked

In 1947 Early Wright became the first African American disc jockey in the South.

the music and arranged for a local flour company, King Biscuit Flour, to sponsor a fifteen-minute live blues program. The band became known as the King Biscuit Entertainers and also included guitarist Robert Lockwood Jr., pianist Pinetop Perkins, and drummer James Curtis Peck. Beginning in November 1941 the musicians were broadcast each day at 12:45 p.m.

The Black Spot on the Dial

To compete with Helena, a West Memphis, Arkansas, station started a broadcast over KWEM with other upcoming and established blues greats, including Howlin' Wolf and Elmore James. Other stations also employed blacks on the other side of the microphone as disc jockeys. For example, in 1947, Early Wright became the first African American disc jockey in the South. In radio, the disc jockey was a star, a well-known and often respected personality. For that person to be black was a significant step forward for African Americans in the American entertainment business.

Then, in 1949, WDIA in Memphis, Tennessee, became the first all-black programmed and hosted station. White-owned, WDIA had gone through a number of format changes in the 1940s without gaining a sustainable audience. However, with its first black disc jockey, high school music teacher Nat Williams, and predominantly blues format, the station became popular. It became even more so when young B.B. King joined as a disc jockey, often playing along on his electric guitar. During the 1950s, WDIA became known as the Black Spot on the Dial—the place where you could tune in and always hear music played by and for African Americans.

WDIA drew numerous musicians from the delta to Memphis, where many like B.B. King became stars. The power of WDIA's transmitter allowed

Blues legend B.B. King plays a riff on his guitar in 1969. As a young man, King was a disc jockey on the popular radio station WDIA in Memphis.

the musicians to reach a greater number of listeners than even the best-selling phonograph records had done. Many of the musicians were so popular that they toured a circuit of nightclubs and theaters throughout the country. Informally known as the Chitlin Circuit (*chitlin* is slang for chitterling, or pig intestines, which was a popular African American dish), the musicians visited cities such as Oakland, New York, and Detroit, beginning in the late 1950s.

Memphis

WDIA also added further acclaim and notoriety to the already burgeoning Memphis blues scene during the 1940s and 1950s. Memphis was among the oldest and most influential blues cities in the South. A popular vaudeville city that often hosted female classic blues performers, Memphis had had the blues for many decades and the blues culture there had been responsible for the rise of two distinct early country blues styles. These were the jug band—folk music played on makeshift instruments such as ceramic jugs and washboards—and the influential and innovative division of lead and rhythm guitars. In this arrangement, instead of one guitarist providing both rhythm and melody, one guitarist strums for the rhythm while the other picks out the melody on individual strings. This arrangement is now standard in many blues and rock bands.

The center of blues in Memphis was Beale Street, which for decades had been a lively, raucous sporting center.

Abundant illicit activity such as bootlegging, prostitution, and gambling was accompanied by a rich blues scene. Music flowed from every door until five or six in the morning. By the 1940s, to many musicians, going to Memphis's Beale Street was an important cultural experience. WDIA DJ Rufus Thompson said that if you came from the delta, as many visiting musicians did, "it was heaven. . . . If you were black for one night on Beale Street, you'd never want to be white no more."[44]

The Blues Relocates

By the 1940s, however, many southern cities such as St. Louis were losing more blues musicians than they were gaining. Even many of the most famous of the Memphis musicians left after gaining stardom, as the center of the blues shifted to the North as part of the Great Migration. This Great Migration, which had begun around the turn of the century, would last until the 1960s, peaking in the 1950s. Although migration slacked off during the Great Depression, during World War II and afterward, jobs in large northern and western cities were plentiful. Innovations in mechanized farming caused many southern agricultural jobs traditionally held by blacks to disappear. During this period hundreds of thousands of blacks moved out of the South to cities like New York, Los Angeles, Houston, Detroit, and particularly Chicago.

The impact of this migration on the country's culture was immense, and it also helped transform the blues into an

Blues and Jazz

As Paul Oliver describes in this excerpt from his book Blues Off the Record, *the development of blues and jazz took place at the same time, but with the blues influencing jazz far more than the other way around.*

As an art form—or art forms—jazz music has developed more or less concurrently with the blues and has been continually fed and revitalized by it. It was the blues that sparked jazz into life, that separated it from the music of the street parade or the ragtime pianist. And if there is any common factor that unites the widely divergent forms of jazz that have originated, flourished, and in some instances already died . . . it is the continued stimulation of the blues. How he plays the blues, his instrumental adaptation of the vocal blues, is still the criterion by which a jazz musician of almost any school is evaluated.

If jazz has depended on the blues for one of its essential qualities, the opposite is not the case. The blues has been influenced very little by jazz: few blues singers are aware of jazz musicians and their music, except as important figures who have made their way in a predominantly white world. . . . But if jazz had never existed the blues would have flourished very well without it.

---

urban music. Despite the fact that the blues had been in urban areas for decades and city styles had become popular, until this period, the home of the blues had remained the rural South. However, as scholar Jon Michael Spencer writes, during this period, blues became dramatically more influential in the cities as greater numbers of black musicians and listeners moved to them: "Although the South would always remain the spiritual home of the blues, Chicago, due to the steady influx of Delta musicians, became the blues capital of the north." [45]

Chicago

Founded by a black trader from Santo Domingo in 1790, Chicago has a long and rich black history. During the nineteenth century, its population grew from one hundred in 1830 to more than one hundred thousand in 1860, with about one thousand African Americans as its residents. The city was an active anti-slavery city in the years leading up to and during the Civil War, and because of this it gained a reputation among white racists as a "nigger loving town." [46] As political activist and historian Dick Gregory notes, the racially tolerant policies of Chicago's politicians were exchanged for black voters' political loyalty: "Chicago was a town where [blacks] could come and survive because Chicago held out a political hand to black folks because it was building a dynasty on black political muscle."[47]

However, despite its reputation as friendly toward blacks, during the early twentieth century, the large number of northward-migrating rural blacks from the South, as well as a large influx of Jews fleeing persecution in Eastern Europe and settling in Chicago, led the white-dominated city government to try to separate blacks and immigrants from white Americans. By the time of World War I, black and Jewish populations had been restricted to living in strictly demarcated ghettos on the south and west sides of the city.

Notwithstanding the segregation, the migration to Chicago never completely stopped and in fact boomed again around the time of World War II, creating another 77 percent increase in Chicago's black population. Most of these blacks were from the Deep South, particularly the Mississippi Delta. So many African Americans from Mississippi left for Chicago and other points north that for the first time in over a cen-

Chicago's famed Maxwell Street bustles with activity in 1939. The street was a cultural center for blacks where the blues thrived.

tury, whites outnumbered blacks in Mississippi. By the 1940s there were more former residents of Mississippi living in the city of Chicago than in any other place in the country, including big southern cities such as Memphis and St. Louis.

Chicago Blues in the 1930s

Many music scholars protest versions of Chicago's blues history that ignore the city's active blues scene prior to the arrival of the urban blues. In fact, with so many delta musicians traveling north during the early decades of the century, Chicago was one of the first northern cities to develop a blues scene.

During the late 1930s, Chicago's blues scene was active and dominated by musicians such as Sonnyboy Williamson I, Big Bill Broonzy, Memphis Minnie, Tampa Red, and others. It was also a popular destination for Delta blues musicians who traveled there to record and then returned home.

The blues center of Chicago was Maxwell Street, a south-side thoroughfare that had become an impromptu street market after the 1871 fire that burned much of the city. By the late 1930s and early 1940s, it was a bustling cultural center, with blues musicians busking (playing for donations) along the street, many with the cords from their electric guitars running into nearby buildings.

Muddy Waters

Though Chicago had a lively blues scene before the urban blues period, the city did not become renowned for its blues until the 1940s and 1950s, when a musician named McKinley Morganfield—better known as Muddy Waters—came to town. Waters helped pioneer the new urban blues sound that became known as the Chicago blues.

A contemporary of Robert Johnson, Waters was a delta-born guitarist who worked on a farm and as a truck driver for many years and came to fame late in life. Influenced by Johnson, Charley Patton, and many other Delta country blues greats, Waters arrived in Chicago in the early 1940s and played and recorded with pianist Sunnyland Slim. Country playing was out of fashion in most cities, and yet that was what he knew best. So Waters adapted Delta country blues to the electric guitar, adding the accompaniment of bass, drums, and harmonica to form the Muddy Waters Blues Band. Waters became one of the first great electric blues guitarists and many believe he pioneered this new modified Delta sound into the Chicago urban blues. He said, "I think I'm responsible for Chicago Blues. I think I set Chicago up for the Blues."[48]

Waters's combination of a rough and raw Delta style with the urban sound of his band was a welcome sound to the numerous delta transplants in the city. His blues, like the Delta blues but unlike the upbeat sophisticated urban styles, was about the vagaries and harsh conditions of urban living. Despite the promise Chicago had held out to migrants, life was hard in the city, just as it had been in the country. Only the details were different. One historian says,

> Musically the Blues has evolved a long way from the songs like [field hollers and jump-ups] but times have remained the same. . . . The hard times people had wanted to leave in Mississippi were still with them in Chicago.[49]

This gritty urban blues caught on in other cities around the country, including Houston and Detroit, where it was picked up by John Lee Hooker, one of the most famous guitarists ever recorded. However, no other city felt the force of this urban blues the way Chicago did.

Jump Blues

At the same time that the small-band, guitar-dominated Chicago blues sound was on the rise, during the mid- to late 1940s, some of the most popular new urban blues music was an early big-band style known as jump blues. Evolving out of the jazz influences of New York from the 1920s onward as well as the swinging piano- and horn-dominated city styles from places like St. Louis and Kansas City, jump blues was a celebratory, swinging, and swaggering music characterized by passionately shouted lyrics, horns, driving boogie-woogie rhythms, and frequent jazz-influenced musical improvisation.

The makeup of a jump blues band was usually a vocalist backed by a medium to large orchestra composed of multiple horns such as saxophones,

Melding electric guitar with Delta blues, Muddy Waters pioneered the gritty sound of Chicago blues.

trumpets, and trombones—with the tenor saxophone often taking the lead—and a piano. The guitar, so important to earlier blues, was demoted to a position in the rhythm section.

Among the best known of the musicians involved in jump blues were Big Joe Turner, Louis Jordan, Louis Prima, Ike Turner, Percy Mayfield, Johnny Otis, and many others working in cities in the Midwest, on the East Coast, and in Los Angeles, which became a home for urban styles of jump blues and the jazzy and piano-based regional style known as West Coast blues. Further, scholars say that the driving rhythm, intense lyrics, and other elements mark jump blues as an early predecessor of rock and roll and an influential forerunner of rhythm and blues.

Rhythm and Blues

The term "rhythm and blues," or R&B, was introduced by *Billboard* magazine in 1949 as a marketing term to replace the 1920s expressions "race music" and "race recording," which many people considered offensive. The music to which it gave its name during the 1940s and 1950s evolved out of a mix of influences, including jump blues, jazz, and black gospel music.

Compared to jump blues, R&B used similar but fewer instruments and there was little improvisation. Formally, it was more basic than jump blues and jazz, featuring an unrelenting backbeat rhythm played along with simpler three-chord melodies that harkened back to older blues. Vocals were central, with the song lyrics taking precedence.

As with jump blues, scholars say that R&B laid the foundation for rock and roll. In fact, an R&B song recorded in Memphis in 1951 is considered by

Sounds for the Big Band Era

Music scholars see the city sounds of boogie-woogie and jump blues as important stylistic developments in the blues, not only in themselves but in that they impacted white musicians and the popular music of big-band swing in the early 1940s.

The blues boogie-woogie sound of the late 1930s inspired swing artists such as Tommy Dorsey and the Andrews Sisters. Dorsey's song "Boogie Woogie" and the Andrews Sisters' "Boogie Woogie Bugle Boy" became hits in the early 1940s and in turn helped inspire more artists to pick up the boogie-woogie sound.

Many musicologists also see jump blues as a stylistic bridge between the older small-band styles of the blues and the big-band sounds that prevailed in the 1940s. The influence of jump blues sounds was so great on swing artists that the renowned King of Swing, white bandleader Benny Goodman, made the risky but ultimately successful decision to bring black jump blues musicians into his band during this period and to incorporate the sound into his music.

many to be the first rock and roll song ever made.

Sun Records

Memphis had been a recording center since the late 1920s, but one of the best-known and most important recording studios for the blues, independent label Sun Records, was not started until 1949. First known as the Memphis Recording Service, Sun Records was the brainchild of its founder and owner, local disc jockey Sam Phillips.

Phillips had grown up with a love for black music, particularly the blues. Living in Memphis, he was aware of the abundance of African American musical talent that was not being recorded, so he decided to do it himself.

Although he was not the only or the first white record producer to record black artists, Phillips ran into a lot of entrenched racist attitudes from other whites in Memphis when he began his business. Nonetheless, he believed that music could serve as a bond between the races. He recalled:

They could not understand why I was out here foolin' around with a bunch of niggers—that's the way they talked. I was just saying we've got to develop something that's good and at the same time could

In 1949 Sam Phillips, a Memphis disc jockey, founded the prominent blues recording label Sun Records.

Bill Haley and His Comets perform at a London theater in 1957. Haley fused elements of rockabilly and R&B, creating rock and roll.

possibly have an elevating effect on what humanity thinks of each other. [50]

During the early 1950s, Phillips recorded many black blues and R&B musicians. However, his work was largely unknown outside the blues community. Then, in 1951, Sun Records quietly made music history when R&B artist Ike Turner and his band, the Kings of Rhythm, recorded "Rocket 88." Described by musical historian Robert Palmer as "a rocking little automobile blues," [51] the song is acknowledged by many as the first rock and roll recording. The record immediately became popular, rising to the top of the R&B sales charts that year and becoming the only song recorded in the South to make it to number one that year.

White Adaptations

The success and sound of R&B songs like "Rocket 88" inspired a white East Coast musician and disc jockey named Bill Haley. Haley, who would go on to rock and roll fame with his song "Rock Around the Clock" a few years later, was the leader of a jazz and country, or "rockabilly," band called the Saddlemen in 1951. They recorded a cover of "Rocket 88," becoming the first in a line of white musicians to adapt R&B songs before the term "rock and roll" was applied to such music.

The first person to call white adaptation of R&B "rock and roll" was Ohio disc jockey Alan Freed, who played R&B for white and black listeners alike. The terms "rock" and "roll" had been used for decades in the blues as a euphemism for sex, and when applied to this driving new music, it became increasingly popular.

Rock and Roll

Despite their popularity with black audiences, purer blues musicians such as Muddy Waters and B.B. King were virtually unknown among white audiences. However, a growing number of young white listeners turned on to white artists like Bill Haley who covered R&B songs. Phillips understood that he could truly establish this new music if he could record a captivating young white star covering R&B songs.

In 1954 a Memphis delivery truck driver named Elvis Presley walked into Sun Records to record a song as a gift for his mother's birthday. After hearing him play, Phillips liked the charismatic, handsome young man's music and asked him to make some more recordings. Out of that session came Presley's first hit and one of the first great rock and roll recordings, "That's All Right Mama," a song written by black blues singer Big Boy Crudup. Presley and other musicians that followed mixed some influences of white country into rhythm and blues and came out with rock and roll.

Thus, while the blues did not create rock and roll, it had more to do with its birth than any other musical style, and scholars say that the influence of rock and roll on American culture is difficult to overstate. In return, in the 1960s, rock and roll had a huge impact on the blues by bringing a new audience—young white listeners—to the music.

Chapter Five

Decline and Revival of the Blues

During the late 1950s and early 1960s, as rock and roll captivated white audiences, the blues-derived music of R&B and its own offshoot, soul, became increasingly popular and took black audiences away from the more traditionally based Chicago-style urban blues. This decline greatly affected the blues culture, particularly those like Muddy Waters, B.B. King, and others, who had electrified and adapted the country blues styles such as Delta blues. While many of these blues musicians continued to play in that vein, others shifted into R&B and soul, while still others left the performing and recording life.

However, during the early 1960s, the traditional blues was resuscitated by two unexpected groups: white folk music enthusiasts interested in reviving the old country styles and white British musicians who had been influenced by the great performing and recording artists of hard, gritty Chicago-style blues during the 1950s. These groups helped breathe new life into the blues and bring it to a new audience of young, white Americans and Europeans. Thus, this period is known among blues fans and scholars as the 1960s Blues Revival.

Soul

The early 1950s were the glory days for the urban blues. The Chicago blues of Muddy Waters in particular dominated the radio, and musicians such as B.B. King crisscrossed the country playing to sold-out, predominantly black crowds. Even country-style guitarists like Texas bluesman Lightnin' Hopkins, who played both the acoustic and electric guitar, became stars. Hopkins recalled, "Jobs wasn't hard to get. . . . Good money too. You could go anywhere, any day and get a job; nothing to worry about too much."[52]

However, as the decade progressed, the blues began to lose favor with its younger black audience, who considered themselves too sophisticated for the blues. These listeners were more interested in R&B and a new music called soul.

Soul was based in the traditions of R&B and black gospel music. Black gospel, which had entered its own golden era in the 1940s, was widely popular in black churches—the music in many cases was considered as important as the sermons. As was true of many of the earliest blues musicians, many of the first African American soul stylists had grown up with a strong church background, many playing the piano or singing in the choir on Sundays.

For decades, the blues and black church music had influenced one another to varying degrees. Even the hard-blues-playing Muddy Waters claimed that you could not truly play the blues without the influence of the church and its music. Gospel and the blues had both been influenced by the early black spirituals, and the two forms of music often shared the same audience—the men and

Ray Charles, shown here at the 1983 Kool Jazz Festival, revolutionized American music when he fused gospel music with R&B.

women who filled the bars and juke joints on Saturday nights were the same people who filled the pews in the churches the next morning (often without much sleep—or any at all—between the two events). However, the two genres of music never melded to a great extent until the 1950s, when a blind pianist named Ray Charles was searching for a new, original sound for his act.

Charles was born in Georgia in 1930 and became blind from glaucoma at the age of seven. Educated in music at the Saint Augustine School for the Deaf and the Blind, Charles was orphaned in his early teens and worked as a musician in Florida and then in Seattle, Washington, in the late 1940s. His first recordings were R&B derivatives or covers of music by Charles Brown and his idol, Nat King Cole. "[I] ate and drank Nat King Cole,"[53] he recalled. Although his recordings were good and he had a couple of R&B hits, it was not until he started infusing his music with gospel that he gained real recognition. He mixed the worldly lyrics of the blues tradition with the fervent energy and earnest, pleading vocals and moans of gospel, and set it to the energetic piano, horns, and rhythms of R&B. This mix of secular and spiritual music made many in the church community unhappy; some claimed that Charles was committing blasphemy by adapting gospel and playing it in clubs and juke joints. However, Charles continued to play the music to great reception. Although it would be a few years before this music was called soul, Charles scored his first hit in this new breed of music with "What'd I Say," which was his first top-ten hit in 1959.

Civil Rights Era

In part, the fervor for the new music was encouraged by the social and political context of African Americans during the mid-1950s to mid-1960s. This period is known as the civil rights era.

Many historians mark the start of the civil rights era with the 1954 U.S. Supreme Court decision in the case of *Brown v. Board of Education*, in which the Court declared racial segregation of public schools to be unconstitutional. From 1954 to 1965, when President Lyndon B. Johnson signed the Voting Rights Act in an effort to enforce voting rights for blacks in southern states, a series of legal challenges, actions of organized civil disobedience, marches, and other measures were undertaken by African Americans who sought to fight discrimination and racial violence and to change white American attitudes toward blacks. Many of these actions, such as the Montgomery, Alabama, bus boycott in 1955, were organized through black churches and supported by black religious leaders, most famously Martin Luther King Jr. Thus, the soundtrack for this era was founded in spirituals and gospel, and scholars say that the importance of this spiritual music helped popularize secularized soul music. Historian Fred J. Hay writes,

Soul music was the music of the Civil Rights movement: soul songs

Civil rights demonstrators march on the Alabama State Capitol in Montgomery in March 1965. Soul music became entwined with the black struggle for racial equality.

became anthems and mottoes for social activists, as is the case in the tremendously popular songs of pride—Aretha Franklin's recording of the Otis Redding composition "Respect" and James Brown's militant "Say It Loud, I'm Black and I'm Proud."[54]

During this period, along with Ray Charles, a number of other artists—including other R&B musicians—became soul musicians. These included Sam Cooke, Gladys Knight, Aretha Franklin, James Brown, Bobby Bland, Wilson Picket, Ike and Tina Turner, Percy Sledge, and many others. Soul grew increasingly popular in the late 1950s and early 1960s, supplanting the blues and even R&B as the most popular black music in the country.

Blues on the Decline

The traditionally based urban blues lost much of its audience during this time. As historian Giles Oakley observes, Chicago blues suffered an image problem among many African Americans: "[The Chicago] style of blues fell rapidly from favour after the mid-50's . . . [because of] assumptions among blacks that the blues were 'low-class,' whiskey sodden and from the gutter."[55]

New, young musicians who had grown up on the blues and drawn influence from the music worked in other genres of music. Those who did not go into R&B or soul were often adopted into white-dominated rock and roll, including black performers such as Chuck Berry and Little Richard.

The loss of popularity was felt by recording artists and producers, as well as performers such as B.B. King, who made their living by touring. King recalls going into a club in Baltimore during the late 1950s and for the first time in his career being booed by the

The King of the Blues

As biographer Bill Dahl writes in the All Music Guide to the Blues, *delta-born blues musician Riley B. "B.B." King overcame humble beginnings to become universally hailed as the reigning king of the blues—a position he has held since the 1950s. Despite his fame and wealth, King remained a modest, gracious man.*

B.B. King is without a doubt the single most important guitarist of the last half century. A contemporary blues solo without a couple of recognizable King-inspired bent notes is all but unimaginable, and he remains a supremely confident singer capable of wringing every nuance from any lyric. . . .

Yet B.B. King remains an intrinsically humble superstar, an utterly accessible icon who welcomes visitors into his dressing room with self-effacing graciousness. Between 1951 and 1985, King notched an amazing 74 entries on *Billboard's* R&B charts, and he was one of the few full-fledged blues artists to score a

major pop hit when his 1970 smash "The Thrill Is Gone" crossed over to mainstream success. . . .

King's immediately recognizable guitar style, utilizing a trademark trill that approximates the bottleneck sound . . . has long set him apart from his contemporaries. Add his patented pleading vocal style and you have the most influential and innovative bluesman of the postwar period.

Showing no signs of slowing down, the king of blues B.B. King performs onstage in April 2005.

black audience. He recalls that it made him feel rejected, saying, "It was like being black twice."[56]

King's experience was not unique, and although the blues did not completely die out, the nationwide popularity it had enjoyed in the late 1940s and early 1950s had definitely waned. In the black clubs and juke joints, the blues continued to progress, but only in cities like Chicago, which had a very strong traditional urban blues culture, did the blues remain a strong force during these years.

During this period, many blues musicians could no longer make a living. Some changed what they played, taking up jazz, country, and other genres of music; however, many quit, and a few disappeared completely from the music scene.

Crossing the Atlantic

At the same time that the blues was on the decline in the United States, the music was experiencing great popularity among a new audience in an unlikely place: Great Britain. As music scholar Bruce Eder writes, like the popularity of rock and roll, the recognition of the blues in Britain was unusual because the music was an American phenomenon: "Great Britain coming into the 20th century had no blues tradition or any basis for it. Blues in Britain was an American import, much the same as rock & roll, but predating it by a few years."[57]

Blues-influenced jazz and big-band music had become popular in Britain and other countries in Europe in the 1920s through the 1940s. Further, like rock and roll recordings during the 1950s, recordings of blues musicians had influenced British popular culture and inspired the development of numerous enthusiasts. However it was not until 1951 that the first blues musician of note, Mississippi-born Chicago blues great Big Bill Broonzy, appeared in England.

Broonzy was brought over by a group of British jazz musicians dedicated to American blues: Alex Korner, Cyril Davies, and Chris Barber. They arranged for Broonzy to perform, and, to his great surprise, he was treated even better in Britain than he had been during the height of popularity of his style of blues in America. There were many opportunities to perform, the money was better than in America, and the audiences, while smaller, were extremely dedicated to the music.

Broonzy's success inspired a string of other blues greats to perform in the UK in the years to come. These included Sonnyboy Williamson II, Howlin' Wolf, Nina Simone, and Muddy Waters. As the popularity of the blues grew in the UK, so did the number of fans, which grew into the thousands.

As British producers and booking agents realized the market potential for the music, the blues became big business in the UK and Europe as festivals, tours, and recordings were arranged. Beginning in 1952, the first American Folk Blues Festival toured through Europe, featuring Muddy Waters, Sonnyboy Williamson II, and Howlin' Wolf. It was extremely lucrative for the performers, and the conditions were so good for American blues musicians that some of them remained in Britain or Europe, particularly as the blues began to suffer in popularity in the United States.

British Blues

As in the United States, many of the most dedicated blues fans were musicians themselves. As the clubs attracted more blues greats, they became increasingly popular with white musicians, who would go to clubs to watch Broonzy, Waters, and others. They learned from them, and often joined in playing with them. Eric Clapton, who eventually became an important blues and rock figure in the UK and the United States, recalls the experience of playing alongside Muddy Waters, one of his longtime blues idols. "I was gobsmacked," he says. "I could hardly move." [58]

Many of these older black blues musicians began recording with English rock and roll bands such as the Yardbirds, the Moody Blues, and the Animals, as well as touring with them. The power of the blues on the British musical scene during the late 1950s and early 1960s heavily influenced British blues musicians, including members of the Beatles, Cream, and the Rolling Stones,

The Beatles appear on the Ed Sullivan Show in 1964. The band was heavily influenced by blues musicians such as Big Bill Broonzy.

the last of which had named their band after the 1951 Muddy Waters Chicago blues hit "Rollin' Stone." These bands performed straightforward or adapted covers of their favorite blues tunes, spreading the popularity of the music throughout Britain.

Taking It Back to the States

Several of the most admired blues-influenced rock bands from Britain—particularly the Beatles, the Rolling Stones, and Cream—became extremely popular in America in the 1960s during what is commonly called the British Invasion. Music scholars claim that the British Invasion of English bands, particularly the Beatles, significantly altered the course of rock and roll history in America. Overtaking the more rockabilly and R&B-rooted rock and roll in popularity, these bands not only brought new, so-called mod haircuts and British accents to rock and roll, they also reinvested the harder blues traditions, lyrics, and styles into the music.

The bands played covers of blues songs, some of whose traditions went back to Delta country roots. They also often invited bluesmen onstage to accompany them or played double-billed concerts with blues musicians. Several bands also recorded blues-dominated albums. Most prominently, in 1964 the Rolling Stones recorded a blues album with Chess Records in Chicago, which during the 1950s had been known for its strong Chicago blues lineup, including Muddy Waters and Howlin' Wolf.

Folk Revival

At the same time as the British were reinvigorating the blues, European and American folk music enthusiasts were helping rediscover some of the music's oldest and greatest living talents. During the 1950s and 1960s, folk music of many kinds experienced a resurgence in Europe and America. Popular young white artists such as Bob Dylan, Joan Baez, and others turned to traditional music as an alternative to increasingly commercialized popular music.

Folk festivals such as the Newport Folk Festival in Rhode Island drew large audiences, and in 1963 and 1964, among the musicians to perform were two country Delta bluesmen whose music had not been heard since the 1930s: Mississippi John Hurt and Skip James.

These musicians had recorded in the late 1920s and early 1930s during the craze for rural blues musicians; however, like much of the country blues of their time, their music was all but forgotten when record companies curtailed their recordings during the Depression and with the shift in popularity toward more urban styling during the 1940s and 1950s. Missing the opportunity for fame, Hurt returned to farming and James became a preacher. When these two played the Newport festival to crowds of thousands, they played before more people than they had ever played to in their lives. By many accounts, these country blues performances, such as Skip James performing his original song "Devil Woman Blues," stole the show.

Other folk festivals followed, many of them featuring blues and many of

Race and White Audiences in the 1950s

By the early 1950s, even as racist attitudes toward blacks were prominent in much of the country, R&B experienced a growing new audience among young whites. As Robert Palmer explains in his book Deep Blues, *this important shift in the listening habits of white Americans was first felt around Memphis.*

A massive shift was taking place in the listening habits of young white Americans, and this shift was felt very early in and around Memphis. Whites in the area had been hiring black entertainers for their school dances, country club parties, plantation cookouts, and other festivities for decades, and, by the beginning of the fifties, most of the jukeboxes in the recreation parlors, soda fountains, swimming pool club rooms, and other spots frequented by white teenagers were stocked almost exclusively with records by black artists. Country and western music was for countrified, lower-class kids. The teenagers who considered themselves sophisticates danced and drank and necked to a soundtrack of "nigger music."

Sam Phillips remembers that at the time "distributors, jukebox operators, and retailers knew that white teenagers were picking up on the *feel* of the black music. These people liked the plays and the sales they were getting, but they were concerned: 'We're afraid our children might fall in love with black people,' [they said]."

---

them influencing young, white American musicians such as Janis Joplin, Bonnie Raitt, and others.

New Blues Audience

The British Invasion and the folk revival both introduced massive white audiences to blues musicians and their songs, creating a resurgence in interest and recordings. A number of older country blues artists, including Son House, Furry Lewis, Skip James, and Mississippi John Hurt, became extremely popular and suddenly found it easy to make a living from performing.

Many of the blues greats of the 1920s and 1930s made numerous recordings during the 1960s and became famous.

Additionally, because of the improvements in recording technologies since the early part of the century, the recordings are still available, whereas many recordings made in the 1920s and 1930s were lost, destroyed, or worn out.

The resurgent popularity of the blues was unexpected, not only because some of the newly popular songs had been written early in the twentieth century, but because of the audience they were reaching. Until the 1960s, the blues had been music played by and to blacks in America; after that time, the audiences were increasingly white.

B.B. King recalls appearing for the first time before a large white audience in San Francisco's Fillmore Theater in 1968. The Fillmore had once been a predominantly black venue, but that night when King walked onstage, he was met with a sea of white faces giving him a three- or four-minute standing ovation, something that had never happened to him before with black audiences. "I almost started to cry,"[59] he recalls. That was the beginning of the second half of his career, playing the blues to a new, white audience.

Many critics and music scholars have tried to explain the appeal of the blues to young, white audiences. Folk music scholar Alan Lomax suggests that whites came to appreciate the blues because the music spoke to hardship and alienation, which in the latter half of the century was increasingly shared by whites. He writes,

The favorite subject of the blues was the trouble between men and women in a disturbed society, and years before the rest of the world, the people of the Delta tasted the bittersweet of modern alienation. So the blues of those days ring true for us now.[60]

Blues Rock

The blues's growing white following made the music a profitable business by the end of the 1960s. This was primarily true for white rock musicians covering and adapting blues into harder rock sounds in a fusion genre known as blues rock. Blues rock was heavily influenced by the Delta/Chicago blues styles of Muddy Waters, Howlin' Wolf, Elmore James, and B.B. King, and was in many ways similar to the Delta/Chicago tradition—except it featured white musicians, louder instruments, bigger amplifiers, and more flamboyant performances.

Blues rock featured young, British blues-influenced bands such as the Rolling Stones, Cream, Fleetwood Mac, Led Zeppelin, John Mayall's Bluesbreakers, Foghat, and the Animals, as well as American bands like the Steve Miller Band, the Allman Brothers, Bob Dylan, the Paul Butterfield Blues Band, and Canned Heat. In the hands of the Allman Brothers, blues rock in turn branched out into the heavily blues-influenced style of rock called Southern rock, and artists such as the Fabulous Thunderbirds, ZZ Top, and

The British group Led Zeppelin adapted Delta and Chicago blues to their own brand of rock to create a wildly popular blues rock sound.

George Thorogood arose from these roots.

The blues in turn borrowed elements from the styles of rock that had developed from blues roots, each genre affecting and being affected by others. By the last decades of the twentieth century, such cross-pollination of the blues, rock, and other genres of music created a great diversity of contemporary styles of blues and blues-influenced music.

Chapter Six

Contemporary Blues

Since its 1960s revival, the blues has become well established in American popular music. A continually developing music in the last decades of the twentieth century and in recent years, the blues has become increasingly diverse in its styles as new artists and elements of rock, country, and other genres of popular music have influenced its evolution and as it has spread around the world. The blues has also changed from it origins and traditions as a music played for and by African Americans to a music with as many white practitioners as black, drawing a predominantly white audience.

Through these changes, the blues has become a highly commercial music. For decades the blues had been the province of small, independent record producers; however, the growing audiences of the 1980s and 1990s drew corporate music companies into marketing the blues. Further, the music inspired franchised chains of blues clubs as well as popular cultural phenomena such as movies and television.

Because of the transformation the blues has gone through during this period, several issues have become subjects of concern within the blues community. For instance, there has been a concerted effort to bring black audiences back to the blues by many musicians and educators who insist that its cultural heritage is important to contemporary African Americans. These developments, changes, and issues regarding the blues have become part of its continuing legacy.

Contemporary Blues Styles

Like most Americans, blues musicians starting out in the 1970s, 1980s, and 1990s—as well as older, established musicians—had listened to a wide variety of popular musical genres, including rock, soul, and country. As a result, borrowed elements from these genres of music found their way into the stylings of the new generation of blues musicians and were picked up as established musicians such as Ray Charles experimented with various forms. From this cross-pollination of the music, fusions such as soul blues, soul rock blues, and country rock blues became increasingly common as individual artists adapted the music to suit their talents and interests. Further, these contemporary styles of blues embraced both acoustic and electric instruments, although acoustic blues remained less popular than electric.

In addition to the diversity of styles, as it continued to spread during the last decades of the twentieth century, the blues adapted to new environments, many of which were outside the United States. During the second half of the twentieth century, it spread through much of the world as blues musicians and blues-influenced rock bands introduced the blues to much of continental

Blues rock musician James Cotton, who learned to play harmonica by imitating Sonnyboy Williamson II, performs at the New Orleans Jazz & Heritage Festival.

Europe and Asia. As blues scholar Robert Palmer writes, "[The blues is] alive in California and New York and London and Paris and Stockholm and Moscow—wherever . . . bluesmen tour and . . . expatriates live, wherever, for that matter, people play or listen to blues-derived rock and roll."[61]

Wherever it was imported, the blues brought a uniquely American music; and as it traveled, it drew local musicians into the blues. European blues musicians, for example, grew in number in this period, including harpist J.J. Milteau, renown as one of the best bluesmen in France, and German blues bands Das Dritte Ohr and Blues Company.

White Blues Musicians

In Europe as in America, since the 1960s, most of the musicians to take up the blues have been white. In fact, among the most significant changes the blues has undergone in the decades since its revival has been the racial makeup of its practitioners and its audience.

Many of the first white blues musicians such as Eric Clapton, the Rolling Stones, Ry Cooder, Bob Dylan, and John Mayall's Bluesbreakers came out of the revival period. In the decades since then a growing number of whites have become renowned for their blues music. While some of these musicians, such as Charlie Musselwhite, Stevie Ray

Russian Blues

The blues spread through much of the world in the latter half of the twentieth century, including Russia. Quoted in Michael Urban's book Russia Gets the Blues, *Russian blues musician Aleksei Agranovskii explains why he and other Russians have embraced the music.*

Why has blues music come to Russia? Well, what we've got in Russia now is just the same thing that existed in the United States when blues first appeared. A big element here is frustration. There are a lot of Russians who feel that they've actually become different people now that the Soviet Union no longer exists. They feel they've become Negroes. Yesterday, they were slaves and our forebears were slaves, too, for many years. People actually feel this. Now what have we got? Well, our freedom, you might say, along with a mass of other problems in which money always seems to figure. Blues is a way to surmount the hang-ups and complexes associated with all that. It is a music that expresses instability and expresses ways in which one can deal with it.

Stevie Ray Vaughan plays a guitar solo behind his head in a 1983 concert. Vaughan was part of the growing number of white musicians since the 1960s who embraced the blues.

Vaughan, and the Fabulous Thunderbirds, were often billed as blues musicians, many blues-influenced artists do not identify themselves as strictly blues musicians and are not marketed as such by their record labels and agents. Instead they are thought of as rock or country musicians who also play blues and who infuse the music with influences from other genres. These musicians include Johnny Cash, Bonnie Raitt, Lucinda Williams, Tom Waits, Nick Cave, Jon Spencer, Cowboy Junkies, the Black Crowes, and many others.

Loss of a Black Audience

As with the racial makeup of those on-stage, blues audiences have become increasingly white. The blues revival of the 1960s was the first introduction of the music to a mass white audience. While many believed that the trend would be short-lived, in the decades since, white blues audiences have continued to grow and dominate. Meanwhile, fewer and fewer blacks have attended blues performances or bought blues recordings.

It remains an open question as to why black audiences turned away from the blues. Some say it was because blacks found R&B and soul more upbeat and danceable than the blues or that, as singer Etta James claims, "most Black people think the blues aren't sophisticated enough."[62] However, some, like journalist Joy Bennett Kinnon, think that there is a stronger reason: The blues serve as an unpleasant reminder of the difficulties of black history in the South and many want to leave the music and the memories behind. Kinnon writes,

> Some experts say that Blacks are ashamed of the blues, which reminds them too much of sharecropping and shanties, cornbread and corn whiskey, and Saturday night juke joints. So they say, Blacks left the blues in the South, abandoned them in Southern fields, scattered like old washtubs by the side of a dusty road.[63]

Additionally, others say that black audiences have not been encouraged to listen to the blues, blaming the scarcity of radio blues programming, which is where most people could be introduced to the music. As recently as the mid-1990s, of the thousands of radio stations in the United States, fewer than fifty featured the blues and most of these were small, college radio stations. Even among all-black format radio stations, few played blues music. Blues musician Robert Cray insists that this situation must change for the blues to remain part of black heritage. He says, "Our black radio stations need to play our music."[64]

Recovering the Blues Heritage

Whatever the reason for the loss of black blues audiences, the change has roused a concern among scholars, critics, musicians, and educators. Many, like Lincoln McGraw Beauchamp, cofounder of the Chicago Blues Artists Coalition, an advocacy group dedicated to preserving the blues, believe that many African Americans are unaware that the blues is the foundation for the contemporary music they love. "A lot of Black people today don't know that the blues is where the music they listen to today comes from. . . . If you study the blues and you listen to rap and Michael Jackson and all this kind of stuff, you learn that what they're doing today can be traced right back [to the blues],"[65] says Beauchamp.

Others see even greater significance to the blues, believing that it is an important part of black cultural heritage in America and among what little African tradition survived slavery. Also, rooted in the storytelling traditions of Africa, the blues contains a musical history, an oral document of black heritage in America. Many, like blues musician Corey Harris, believe that the cultural heritage found in the blues is a vital element of the African American identity.

Harris says, "To know yourself, you have to know the past. And to know where you're going, you have to know where you've been."[66]

Some educators are taking the initiative to bring the blues back to black

White Audiences Changed the Blues

When white audiences discovered the blues in the 1960s, they dramatically changed the course of the music. In the opinion of many, like music critic Joel Selvin in the San Francisco Chronicle, *the change was for the worse.*

Young white Americans were discovering black music, and digging it. This sudden racial shift in the blues audience had catastrophic effects on the music. The black blues musicians found themselves disconnected from their familiar audience. Outside their community, they didn't know what they had to say to this new, white crowd. They didn't trust the audience's ability to understand them, and approached the prospect with well-justified suspicion. Nevertheless, if Lightnin' Hopkins was going to make $1,000 a night playing the down-home Texas blues . . . he was going to be performing for white people and the impact on his art was

substantial. Once the music's original audience evaporated, it was an adjustment every black blues musician had to make.

As long as blues was blacks talking to blacks, it thrived on honesty, lack of artifice, a blunt candor that lay at the heart of the music. It was not show business—it was life and death. . . .

In front of white audiences, they entered the realm of show business. Some couldn't resist playing the clown. . . . Blues became just another musical style that anyone could play. . . .

The blues has always been a protean musical form that supported a wide range of personal expression. Within the typical three-chord progressions, musicologists have traced more than 5,000 variations. But divorced from its cultural context, blues lost its reason to be, its cultural imperative, and, with that, a lot of its sweeping powers.

audiences by introducing school-children to the music. Chicago Blues Artists Coalition cofounder Valerie Wellington brings blues musicians to schools for minirevues and concerts, believing such contact with the blues can build a new black audience. She says:

> We have to start with the children, teaching them about our heritage

. . . . And the blues are a part of that heritage. I find once you expose children to it, they like it, and suddenly you have a new generation of blues fans. [67]

Others, like musician B.B. King, say that whether African American children enjoy the music or not, it is a part of their heritage and they should learn about it. King says,

Rap artists like Talib Kweli (pictured) use their songs to educate listeners about black cultural heritage.

I don't want them to like it. They can like it if they want to, but they should know about it. I just want our kids to know about it. . . . I don't altogether blame them [for not knowing]. I blame us for not making a better effort to know their roots. [68]

Are Whites Taking Over the Blues?

Many in the blues fear that if new generations of blacks do not take an interest in the blues, in one or more generations, whites could be the only musicians carrying on the traditions of the music. Etta James says,

It could happen, and it would be a shame, because blues and jazz are the only forms of music originated in this country and they were both started by blacks. Wouldn't it be something if we gave it away because we didn't recognize it as good music? [69]

This fear is accentuated by the fact that the blues is dying out in parts of the country that once were black blues centers. This is particularly true in the Mississippi Delta, considered by many to be the birthplace of the blues. The few Delta blues musicians who are still alive and playing in the area have witnessed the collapse of a culture brought on by the Great Migration and ultimately the shift of the audience to whites. Journalist Rick Bragg writes:

Here in the Delta, where most of the legendary juke joints have slowly shut their doors and most of the bluesmen have died off or moved away, the blues is fading from the very place it was born, say the people who played it and others who lived here.

They know their music survived, in the music collections of yuppies, in college seminars on folk culture, in festivals and franchised venues . . . in the United States, Asia, and Europe. [70]

Even in places like Memphis, St. Louis, and Chicago, where the blues is still actively played, the old blues haunts like Beale Street and Maxwell Street have become tourist attractions marketed to whites and have lost much of their old spirit.

Many blacks have become angered that whites have become so involved in the blues, seeing it as one of many appropriations of black culture by whites that have occurred over the centuries since African slaves were brought to America. However, as musician Koko Taylor suggests, the whites did not so much take the blues away from blacks as they picked it up when blacks discarded it:

[Blacks] look down on the blues like they're looking at a pile of garbage. Then when the Whites come along, they love it; they're paying for it. And then our people

In 1995 a white man peruses the blues cassettes for sale in a bluesmobile on Chicago's New Maxwell Street, a famous blues haunt.

are the first to say they took our music. Nah, they didn't take it. We gave it to them.[71]

Indeed, whites have taken the lead not only in buying records and show tickets but some have also become most active in blues preservation. Blues scholars, club organizers, and preservation societies in the recent decades have been started and run largely by whites.

Commercialization of the Blues

One of the most significant effects of the rise of white audiences on the blues is that it has made the music more commercial than ever before. This is evident in the way the music is produced, marketed, and performed around the world.

Since the 1920s and 1930s, when many of the big record companies that had blues labels either dropped the blues or went out of business, the blues has largely been produced by small, independent record producers. Several of these labels, such as Sun Records in Memphis and Chess Records in Chicago, were extremely important to the blues boom years of the 1950s. From the 1960s into the 1980s, independents remained dominant, particularly Alligator Records, established in 1970, and San Francisco's Blind Pig Records, established in 1986. The major record-producing companies at the time produced some blues, but mostly in the guise of rock and other more commercially established genres. Until the early 1990s, producers directed blues records toward niche markets such as collectors. Nevertheless, small producers made large sales.

In the 1990s, large, often corporate-owned record companies began taking an interest in the blues because of the profits being made by the independents. Additionally, as journalist Chris Morris writes, the 1990s was another boom period for the blues due to the coincidence of several factors:

> Events as diverse as the success of Detroit blues titan John Lee Hooker's [album] "The Healer" in 1989, the reissue of Delta bluesman Robert Johnson's collected works in 1990, blues-rocker Bonnie Raitt's 1990 Grammy triumph with "Nick of Time" and the posthumous deification of guitarist Stevie Ray Vaughan [who died in a helicopter crash in August 1990] all helped feed the appetites of blues lovers, young and old.[72]

With the introduction of major record producers, the blues became bigger business than it ever had been. The popularity of the blues abroad also created rich markets for the music in other countries, encouraging large foreign and multinational companies to get into the business of selling the blues. Companies in Britain, Austria, Holland, Italy, and France have gotten involved in producing the blues.

Thus, around the world, more records were being made and the competition was making it possible for blues producers and musicians to get rich. Mike Vernon, president of British music producing company Code Blue notes that the blues market has actually become glutted to the point of overwhelming the consumer: "There is so much being released. In the '60's, there was nothing like the material available to

The huge success of John Lee Hooker's 1989 album The Healer *helped to broaden the appeal of blues to white audiences.*

the consumer [now]. . . . We're being barraged, almost, and the buyer can't keep up with it."[73]

One negative side effect of the situation was that, while older established blues musicians like B.B. King, John Lee Hooker, and Ray Charles found it easier to make records and make more money from them, it became harder for the few young blacks who were interested in becoming blues musicians to enter the business because many labels are afraid to risk marketing new artists to audiences that want proven names. In addition to shutting out new black musicians and thus further alienating blacks from the blues, some worry that the blues will become stagnant if new artists are not encouraged to play and adapt the blues. Edward Chmelewski of Blind Pig Records says, "If it doesn't sound like Sonny Boy Williamson, they're not going to like it . . . [but] you don't want [blues] to become a museum piece—it's a living art form, and it's got to grow and change."[74]

Many also worry that the contemporary commercialization of the blues is contrary to the music's spirit. As one journalist writes, "In its self-conscious obsession with style, a desire to reduce experience to a hip post-modernist game, the pop-music spirit of [recent years] may be the antithesis of the blues."[75]

Similarly, commercial outlets, such as the white-owned franchise blues club House of Blues, have come under attack by critics who claim that such businesses cynically appropriate and romanticize the blues out of context of its difficult history. Journalist Daniel Lieberfeld writes:

Because of blues culture's commercialization and accompanying loss of social context, the white imagination ignores or romanticizes the poverty, violence, and endurance that bred and fed the blues. . . . In place of such disconcertingly complex realities, House of Blues proffers a blues theme-park. . . . No one has to go anywhere grimy, hear anyone talking out of their head, or, for that matter, encounter blacks in positions of authority. It's possible to groove along to a song about being Broke and Hongry and Ain't Got a Lousy Dime, and then order another $4.50 beer from one of the club's predominantly white wait-staff.[76]

Blues in Popular Culture

Despite such concerns, others were happy to see the growth in the blues market and its audiences in recent decades. Mel Cramer, the producer and host of the blues radio program *Blues After Hours* on WGBH radio in Boston, says, "What's wonderful about the current scene is more people are listening and joining blues societies."[77]

Indeed, according to music industry experts, in the 1990s and early 2000s, there have been more blues festivals, blues tours, and blues venues than ever

The white-owned franchise blues club House of Blues has a number of locations in cities across the country, including this one in Los Angeles.

before. The blues has also become a force on the Internet, with blues chat groups arising at a rapid pace. "[The blues] is the most popular it has ever been,"[78] says Bruce Iglauer of Alligator Records.

Blues in Film

With the growth in its popularity and its commercial potential, in recent decades the blues has increasingly entered mainstream popular culture outside the music industry, becoming a popular subject for film and television. Among the best known in this regard

was the act known as the Blues Brothers. Created in 1977 by Canadian actor Dan Aykroyd and Chicago actor John Belushi on the popular late-night program *Saturday Night Live,* the Blues Brothers featured Elwood (Aykroyd) and Jake (Belushi) Blues, a pair of black-suited, sunglasses-clad blues musicians who performed blues music and skits on the show. Their act was so popular that they recorded their first album, *Briefcase Full of Blues,* in 1978. The record featured covers of blues songs such as blues great Junior Wells's "Messin' with the Kid."

Aykroyd and Belushi went on to make the feature-length movie *The Blues Brothers* in 1980, reprising their roles as Jake and Elwood Blues along with a supporting cast of blues, R&B, and soul music greats such as Ray Charles, James Brown, and Aretha Franklin. The film was extremely popular and was responsible for introducing large numbers of people to blues music.

A few other notable blues films include *Sounder* (1972), *Crossroads* (1986), and *O Brother, Where Art Thou?* (2000). *Sounder* is the story of a sharecropper family during the Great Depression, which features blues musician Taj Mahal in the cast and music by Lightnin' Hopkins on the soundtrack. *Crossroads* features a young white musician's quest to learn to play the Delta blues, and the

In 1977 Dan Aykroyd (left) and John Belushi created the wildly popular Blues Brothers act, which introduced blues music into mainstream white culture.

Blues: The New Generation

The 2003 Year of the Blues celebrations across America caused New York Times *journalist Jon Parjeles to warn people against thinking of the blues as a nostalgic thing of the past.*

A few younger rockers have made their own discovery of the blues, particularly jam bands and the White Stripes. But most contemporary rock and pop is at least a generation removed from the classic electric blues that inspired musicians like the Rolling Stones, Aerosmith and Bonnie Raitt. . . .

Still, any night of the week, in big cities and rural outposts, blues bands continue to play. . . . In Mississippi, blues and Southern soul are still regular radio fare.

Yet their audience isn't getting any younger. And the blues, once fierce and disquieting music, is often marketed as something comfortable, good for selling jeans and beer. . . .

But the blues should not be a nostalgia trip. The music is imbedded in American and world culture, and it earned its place with beauty and guile, gaining traction with every misreading. Guitar solos and letting the good times roll were part of it, but by no means the whole story. The blues was once as audacious as hip-hop, as intimate as emo and as insubordinate as punk.

story deals with the crossroads legend of blues musicians Tommy Johnson and Robert Johnson selling their souls to the devil in trade for their incredible talents. Like *Sounder, O Brother, Where Art Thou?* is set in Mississippi during the 1930s and portrays a wide array of music from the period, including prison chain gang blues and the Delta blues of Tommy Johnson, who enters the story as a character portrayed by actor Chris Thomas King.

Beyond film portrayals, the blues has been featured in numerous television programs, including *The Cosby Show* in the 1980s and *Arsenio!* in the late 1990s. Further, in film and on television, the study and appreciation of blues has led to numerous concert films and documentaries. Among these are a series of documentary films produced in 2003 by Italian-American director, producer, and blues fan Martin Scorsese. The series, called *The Blues,* features documentaries by several directors, including Scorsese himself, Clint Eastwood, Wim Wenders, and Mike Figgis. Such films, programs, and documentaries have added to the popularity of the music and have also made an increasing impact on the appreciation of the heritage and legacy of the blues.

Legacy of the Blues

The blues continues to evolve to the present day and has become increasingly integrated and commercialized as part of the American mainstream. It has also gained recognition as an important musical form and cultural phenomenon. The year 2003—a century after W.C. Handy famously first heard the Delta blues in a train station in Tutwiler, Mississippi—was dedicated by Congress as the Year of the Blues and celebrated with concerts, documentary films, the release of reissued blues albums, and other events. Whether this trend will ultimately change the blues beyond recognition and transform it into just another genre of popular music remains to be seen. However, the legacy of the blues is evident today, in what it has added to the culture, in its musical influence, and on its greater significance to many of its fans, scholars, and practitioners.

Despite the abandonment of the blues by many blacks in recent decades, the blues is deeply intertwined with African American heritage and culture and remains influential in black music and language. For example, the wordplay involved in the blues, its emphasis on rhythm, and its openness and humor regarding sexuality are the roots of most contemporary black music, including most recently rap and hip-hop. These same elements have also transformed other American musical forms.

Further, the vocabulary of the blues has added numerous phrases to the American idiom, including "the eagle flies on Friday" (meaning payday), "mojo" and "mojo hand" (which were magic spells used in voodoo and hoodoo), "rounder" (meaning a man who gets around or a big-money poker player), and a host of others.

To some, the most significant legacy of the blues is what the music represented—and continues to represent. The blues began as a music of survival to help people through hard times, and, as music scholar Larry Neal notes, the blues are also about finding meaning:

> Blues are basically defiant in their attitude toward life. They are about survival on the meanest, most gut level of human experience. The essential motive behind the best blues song is the acquisition of insight, wisdom. [79]

Further, the blues is about hope, and, as scholar Douglas Henry Daniels writes, that hope is still important in contemporary times:

> From an Afro-American perspective, the nation's history has been characterized by optimistic expectations followed by disappointment. The disappointment produces a blue mood and a situation in which blues can aid in our comprehension of the experience and perhaps help us to arrive at a solution. During [re-

The White Stripes, seen here performing at the 2004 Grammy Awards, are one of the latest rock bands to borrow heavily from the blues.

cent years], any thinking citizen is susceptible to an attack of the blues when he reads the headlines. . . . [Thus, the blues] is particularly relevant for grasping the fact that we can overcome the limitations of our society and the results of our history. . . . [As] an art form developed by slaves and their descendants, [the blues] has a special significance for every citizen who has an enlightened sense of the nation's history and its potential. [80]

From its earliest roots to its most recent incarnation, the adaptability and power of the blues to move people's emotions has made it one of the most influential and permeating genres of music in the country and around the world. Most scholars, fans, and musicians believe that as the blues enters its second century of existence, the issues that threaten and confront it will continue to shape the music and that it will continue to have an impact on American and world music.

• Notes •

Introduction: The Music of Survival

1. Quoted in J.E. Lighter, *Random House Dictionary of American Slang.* New York: Random House, 1994, vol. 1, p. 206.
2. Quoted in *Blues Like Showers of Rain,* produced and directed by John Jeremy. Lyme, CT: Rhapsody Films, 1986.
3. Quoted in *The Blues, a Musical Journey,* part 6: *Red, White, and Blues,* produced and directed by Mike Figgis. New York: Sony Music Entertainment/Columbia Music Video, 2003.
4. Langston Hughes, "Songs Called the Blues," *Phylon,* vol. 36, no. 2 (1941), 143–44.
5. Hughes, "Songs Called the Blues," p. 144.
6. Max Haymes, "Blues Definitions," Early Blues Web site, www.early blues.com/Blues_definitions.htm.
7. Alan Lomax, *The Land Where the Blues Began.* New York: Pantheon, 1993, p. ix–x.

Chapter One: The Origins of the Blues

8. Quoted in Gerhard Kubik, *Africa and the Blues.* Jackson: University Press of Mississippi, 1999, p. 7.
9. Quoted in George Gibson, "Gourd Banjos: From Africa to the Appalachians," Gourd Banjo Web site, www.dhyatt.com/history_3_ colamer.html.
10. Jimpson & ax gang, "No More, My Lord," *Prison Songs,* vol. 1, *Murderous Home.* Green Records, 1997.
11. Marta J. Effinger, "The Struggle and the Dream," *Footsteps,* March/April 2002, p. 8.
12. Quoted in Effinger, "The Struggle and the Dream," p. 8.
13. Effinger, "The Struggle and the Dream," p. 10.
14. Heavenly Midis Songbook, "Go Down Moses," http://my.homewith god.com/heavenlymidis/songbook/ moses.html.
15. Quoted in *Rise and Fall of Jim Crow,* Program 1, *Promises Betrayed,* produced by Sam Pollard. San Francisco: California Newsreel, 2002.

Chapter Two: Country Blues

16. Quoted in Delta Blues Museum, "The Land and the River," www.delta bluesmuseum.org/index.cfm?page= AboutTheDelta&subID=25.
17. Mark Twain, *Life on the Mississippi,* New York: Bantam Classics, 1983, p. 2.
18. Lomax, *The Land Where the Blues Began,* p. 65.

19. Robert Palmer, *Deep Blues*. New York: Viking, 1981, p. 41.

20. Alan Coukell, "Etta Baker, Legend of Piedmont Blues," NPR, March 16, 2005. www.npr.org/templates/story/story.php?storyId=4536802.

21. Richard Newman, "A Tradition Begins," *Footsteps,* March/April 2002, p. 2.

22. Quoted in Oliver, *The Story of the Blues*. Philadelphia: Chilton, 1969, p. 27.

23. Quoted in Oliver, *The Story of the Blues,* p. 32.

24. Palmer, *Deep Blues,* p. 75.

25. Quoted in *Land Where the Blues Began,* produced by Alan Lomax. New York: Phoenix Films, 1980.

26. Lomax, *The Land Where the Blues Began,* pp. xiv–xv.

27. Giles Oakley, *The Devil's Music: A History of the Blues*. London: British Broadcasting Corporation, 1976, p. 61.

28. Quoted in *The Land Where the Blues Began*.

29. Samuel Charters, *The Bluesmen: The Story and the Music of the Men Who Made the Blues*. New York: Oak Publications, 1967, p. 38.

30. Quoted in Charters, *The Bluesmen,* p. 40.

31. Quoted in Oakley, *The Devil's Music,* p. 55.

Chapter Three: Popularization of the Blues

32. Quoted in Oakley, *The Devil's Music,* p. 6.

33. Palmer, *Deep Blues,* p. 105.

34. "Vaudeville! A History," American Studies Department, University of Virginia. http://xroads.virginia.edu/~ma02/easton/vaudeville/vaudeville.html.

35. Quoted in *Essential Blues Masters History of the Blues, Volume 1,* written by Barbara L. Kaye, directed by L.L. Tarter. Los Angeles: Rhino Home Video, 1993.

36. Quoted in Harriet Ottenheimer, "The Blues Tradition in St. Louis," *Black Music Research Journal,* Autumn 1989, p. 137.

37. Jon Michael Spencer "The Diminishing Rural Reside of Folklore in City and Urban Blues, Chicago 1915–1950," *Black Music Research Journal,* Spring 1992, p. 26.

38. Spencer, "The Diminishing Rural Reside of Folklore in City and Urban Blues," p. 26.

39. Quoted in Oakley, *The Devil's Music,* p. 36.

40. Quoted in Vladimir Bogdanov, Chris Woodstra, and Stephen Thomas Erlewine, eds., *All Music Guide to the Blues: The Definitive Guide to the Blues,* 3rd ed. San Francisco: Backbeat Books, 2003, p. xi

41. David Evans, Editor's Introduction, *Black Music Research Journal,* Spring 2000, p. 1.

42. Russell Banks, "The Devil and Robert Johnson: The Blues and the 1990s," *New Republic,* April 29, 1991, p. 27.

Chapter Four: Urban Blues

43. Lomax, *The Land Where the Blues Began,* p. 38.

44. Quoted in *The Blues, a Musical Journey,* part 3: *Road to Memphis,* produced and directed by Richard Pearce. New York: Sony Music Entertainment/Columbia Music Video, 2003.

45. Spencer, "The Diminishing Rural Reside of Folklore in City and Urban Blues," p. 32.

46. Quoted in Palmer, *Deep Blues,* p. 137.

47. Quoted in *Chicago Blues,* produced and directed by Harley Cokliss. Lyme, CT: Rhapsody Films, 1991.

48. Quoted in *Chicago Blues.*

49. Quoted in *The Blues, a Musical Journey,* part 5: *Godfathers and Sons,* produced and directed by Marc Levin. New York: Sony Music Entertainment/Columbia Music Video, 2003.

50. Quoted in *The Blues, a Musical Journey,* Part 5: *Godfathers and Sons.*

51. Palmer, *Deep Blues,* p. 222.

Chapter Five: Decline and Revival of the Blues

52. Quoted in Oakley, *The Devil's Music,* p. 241.

53. Quoted in *The Blues, a Musical Journey,* part 7: *Piano Blues,* produced and directed by Clint Eastwood. New York: Sony Music Entertainment/Columbia Music Video, 2003.

54. Fred J. Hay, "The Sacred/Profane Dialectic in Delta Blues: The Life and Lyrics of Sonny Boy Williamson," *Phylon,* vol. 48, no. 4 (1987), p. 318.

55. Oakley, *The Devil's Music,* p. 244.

56. Quoted in *The Blues, a Musical Journey,* part 6: *Red, White, and Blues.*

57. Bruce Eder, "British Blues," in *All Music Guide to the Blues,* 3rd ed., ed. Vladimir Bogdanov, Chris Woodstra, and Stephen Thomas Erlewine. San Francisco: Backbeat Books, 2003, p. 700.

58. Quoted in *The Blues, a Musical Journey,* part 6: *Red, White, and Blues.*

59. Quoted in *The Blues, a Musical Journey,* part 6: *Red, White, and Blues.*

60. Quoted in *Land Where the Blues Began.*

Chapter Six: Contemporary Blues

61. Palmer, *Deep Blues,* p. 253.

62. Quoted in Joy Bennett Kinnon, "Are Whites Taking or Are Blacks Giving Away the Blues?" *Ebony,* September 1997, p. 86.

63. Kinnon, "Are Whites Taking or Are Blacks Giving Away the Blues?" p. 86.

64. Quoted in Kinnon, "Are Whites Taking or Are Blacks Giving Away the Blues?" p. 86.

65. Quoted in Charles Whitaker, "Are Blacks Giving Away the Blues? White Fans Keep the Music and Its Artists Going Strong," *Ebony,* October 1990, p. 46.

66. Quoted in *The Blues, a Musical Journey,* Part 1: *Feel Like Goin' Home,* produced and directed by Martin Scorsese. New York: Sony Music Entertainment Columbia Music Video, 2003.

67. Quoted in Whitaker, "Are Blacks Giving Away the Blues?" p. 46.

68. Quoted in Kinnon, "Are Whites Taking or Are Blacks Giving Away the Blues?" p. 89.

69. Quoted in Whitaker "Are Blacks Giving Away the Blues?" p. 46.

70. Rick Bragg, "The Blues Is Dying in the Place It Was Born," *New York Times,* April 22, 2001, p. 26.

71. Quoted in Kinnon, "Are Whites Taking or Are Blacks Giving Away the Blues?" p. 91.

72. Chris Morris, "Messin' with the Blues," *Billboard,* June 15, 1996, p. 31.

73. Quoted in Morris, "Messin' with the Blues," p. 31.

74. Quoted in Morris, "Messin' with the Blues," p. 31.

75. *Economist,* "Rebirth of the Blues," May 4, 1996, p. 88.

76. Daniel Lieberfeld, "Million-Dollar Juke Joint: Commodifying Blues Culture," *African American Review,* Summer 1995, p. 220.

77. Quoted in Kirsten A. Conover, "Singing the Blues: America's Original Folk Art That Celebrates the Triumph of the Spirit Is Now More Popular than Ever," *Christian Science Monitor,* November 21, 1996, p. 10.

78. Quoted in Conover, "Singing the Blues," p. 10.

79. Quoted in Jess Tyehimba, "The Word/The Blues. A Meditation. Investigating Blues Poetry, an Oral Tradition," *Black Issues Book Review,* March/April 2004, p. 19.

80. Douglas Henry Daniels, "The Significance of the Blues for American History," *Journal of Negro History,* Winter/Spring 1985, pp. 21–22.

• For Further Reading •

Books

Dan Aykroyd and Ben Manilla, *Elwood's Blues: Interviews with the Blues Legends and Stars.* San Francisco: Backbeat Books, 2004. A collection of interviews with blues musicians contemporary and past conducted by Aykroyd's alter ego, Elwood Blues.

James Ciment, *Atlas of African-American History.* New York: Facts On File, 2001. This atlas covers the history of African Americans from their African origins through the end of the twentieth century. Includes maps, charts, graphs, photos, illustrations, and other aids.

Howard Elmer, *Blues: Its Birth and Growth.* New York: Rosen, 1999. A brief history of the blues from its origins through the 1990s. Includes a glossary and discography.

Hetti Jones, *Big Star Fallin' Mama: Five Women in Black Music,* rev. ed. New York: Viking, 1995. This collection of biographies features five important female blues singers: Ma Rainey, Bessie Smith, Mahalia Jackson, Billie Holiday, and Aretha Franklin. Includes a bibliography and discography, as well as a list of other prominent women in black music.

Alexandria Manera, *Bessie Smith.* Chicago: Raintree, 2003. A brief biography of classic blues singer Bessie Smith. Includes a glossary and time line.

Robert Santelli, *The Big Book of Blues: A Biographical Encyclopedia.* New York: Penguin, 1993. A collection of more than six hundred biographies of musicians involved with the blues and other forms of music influenced by the blues.

Jerry Silverman, *Outlaws and Outcasts.* New York: Chelsea House, 1996. This book contains the sheet music and lyrics for twenty-eight blues songs, including an explanation of each song's origins and the meaning of the lyrics.

L.S. Summer, *W.C. Handy: Founder of the Blues.* Chanhassen, MN: Child's World, 2002. This brief biography of the self-proclaimed Father of the Blues, musician W.C. Handy, includes a time line, glossary, and suggestions for further reading.

Mary Wilds, *Raggin' the Blues: Legendary Country Blues and Ragtime Musicians.* Greensboro, NC: Avisson Press, 2001. This brief collection of biographies includes eight important country blues and ragtime musicians. Includes discography and videography and illustrated portraits of each musician.

Video

Bessie Smith, produced by Warner Amex Satellite Entertainment. Princeton,

NJ: Films for the Humanities, 1988. This biography of classic female blues singer Bessie Smith illustrates her poverty-stricken childhood, her development of the classical blues style, and her early death in an automobile accident.

Big City Blues, produced and directed by St. Clair Bourne. Lyme, CT: Rhapsody Films, 1986. Filmed in Chicago, this history of the blues mixes scenes of the city of Chicago with musical performances and interviews with people connected with the blues.

The Blues, a Musical Journey, part 2: *Soul of a Man,* produced and directed by Wim Wenders. New York: Sony Music Entertainment/Columbia Music Video, 2003. This film explores the lives of bluesmen Skip James, Blind Willie Johnson, and J.B. Lenoir through a fictional film-within-a-film, rare archival footage, and covers of their songs by contemporary musicians.

The Blues, a Musical Journey, part 4: *Warming by the Devil's Fire,* produced and directed by Charles Burnett. New York: Sony Music Entertainment/Columbia Music Video, 2003. Mixing fiction with documentary, this film presents the tale of a young boy's encounter with his family in Mississippi in the 1950s and intergenerational tensions between gospel and the blues.

John Lee Hooker: That's My Story, produced and directed by Jörg Bundschuh. New York: New Video Group, 2003. This documentary tells the story of blues legend John Lee Hooker, a teenage runaway who never went to school and spent years working in a factory before becoming one of the most prolific blues artists of all time.

The Search for Robert Johnson, produced and directed by Chris Hunt. New York: SMV Enterprises, 1992. This video traces the life of Robert Johnson, based on extensive research by the filmmakers into this private, troubled figure. Includes interviews with fellow bluesmen who knew Johnson as well as one of his former girlfriends.

Web Site

Gourd Banjo Web site (www.dhyatt. com). This Web site is the home of David G. Hyatt, an enthusiast and maker of gourd banjos. The site includes an eight-part historical feature on the history and use of the instrument, including the banjo during the period of slavery.

• Works Consulted •

Books

Amiri Baraka [Leroi Jones], *Blues People: Negro Music in White America.* New York: Morrow Quill, 1963. A history of jazz and the blues that attempts to place the events and figures in their historical and social context. This was among the first works of this kind written by an African American.

William Barlow and Cheryl Finley, *From Swing to Soul: An Illustrated History of African American Popular Music from 1930 to 1960.* Washington, DC: Elliott & Clark, 1994. This book traces the blues and its influence on other African American music such as swing, R&B, jazz, and soul as they developed during the 1930s and through the 1960s.

Vladimir Bogdanov, Chris Woodstra, and Stephen Thomas Erlewine, eds., *All Music Guide to the Blues: The Definitive Guide to the Blues.* 3rd ed. San Francisco: Backbeat Books, 2003. An encyclopedic guide to blues history, blues artists, and blues recordings. Includes music maps showing musical lineages and essays describing various blues styles and important events as well as reviews of thousands of blues albums.

Samuel Charters, *The Bluesmen: The Story and the Music of the Men Who Made the Blues.* New York: Oak Publications, 1967. This book provides regional histories, biographies, and studies of the music of important early blues musicians from Mississippi, Alabama, and Texas.

———, *The Roots of the Blues: An African Search.* Boston: Marion Boyars, 1981. Part blues exploration and part travelogue, this book recounts the author's voyage to Africa to study the origins of the blues.

Steve Cheseborough, *Blues Traveling: The Holy Sites of Delta Blues.* Jackson: University Press of Mississippi, 2001. An in-depth travel guide to important sites of the Delta blues, including contemporary landmarks, festivals, and grave markers of famous blues musicians.

James Dickerson, "British Blues," in *All Music Guide to the Blues.* 3rd ed. Ed. Vladimir Bogdanov, Chris Woodstra, and Stephen Thomas Erlewine. San Francisco: Backbeat Books, 2003.

———, *Goin' Back to Memphis: A Century of Blues, Rock 'n' Roll, and Glorious Soul.* New York: Schirmer, 1996. This musical history of Memphis emphasizes the city's importance in the development of the blues, rock and roll, and soul.

Julio Finn, *The Bluesman: The Musical Heritage of Black Men and Women in the Americas.* New York: Interlink, 1992. This book is an in-depth analysis of the African roots of the blues, including religion, social elements of African culture, and instruments. Includes a glossary of important African terms.

Jackie Kay, *Bessie Smith*. Bath, Somerset, UK: Absolute Press, 1997. Part of the Outlines series, this brief, creative biography of Bessie Smith examines her life and career while interweaving poetry, fiction, and biography throughout.

Gerhard Kubik, *Africa and the Blues*. Jackson: University Press of Mississippi, 1999. This book focuses on the musicological aspects of the blues and their relation to African antecedents, cultures, and practices.

J.E. Lighter, *Random House Dictionary of American Slang*. Vol. 1. New York: Random House, 1994. This three-volume reference provides historic and contemporary definitions and examples of american colloquial language.

Alan Lomax, *The Land Where the Blues Began*. New York: Pantheon, 1993. A detailed account of the author's historic field expedition in the 1940s, during which he recorded folk and blues music throughout the Deep South.

Giles Oakley, *The Devil's Music: A History of the Blues*. London: British Broadcasting Corporation, 1976. This study of the blues begins with the period of slavery and ends in the years following World War II. Includes numerous photographs, a discography, bibliography, and index of songs.

Paul Oliver, *Blues Fell This Morning: Meaning in the Blues*. 2nd ed. New York: Cambridge University Press, 1990. In this study, the author analyzes many blues lyrics in depth, examining their historical, political, and social contexts.

———, *Blues Off the Record: Thirty Years of Blues Commentary*. New York: Hippocrene, 1984. This collection of essays and criticism on the blues provides historical and background information on the genre as well as in-depth looks at particular aspects of blues music, history, and culture.

———, *The Story of the Blues*. Philadelphia: Chilton, 1969. This history of the blues includes numerous essays on the development of the genre, its figures, and the social context of the music. Includes numerous black-and-white photographs and illustrations of the periods discussed.

Jim O'Neal and Amy Van Singel, *The Voice of the Blues: Classic Interviews from* Living Blues Magazine. New York: Routledge, 2002. Includes transcripts of interviews with a dozen important blues musicians, including Muddy Waters.

Robert Palmer, *Deep Blues*. New York: Viking, 1981. Through historical narrative and anecdotal examples, this book details the history of the blues from its roots in the Deep South through the 1950s and 1960s.

Jeff Todd Titon, *Early Downhome Blues: A Musical and Cultural Analysis*. 2nd ed. Chapel Hill: University of North Carolina Press, 1994. A musical study of traditional blues artists and their songs. Includes musical analysis and cultural history of the early period of the blues. Includes an appendix on patterns of blues record purchasing and listening.

Mark Twain, *Life on the Mississippi*. New York: Bantam Classics, 1983. Twain's memoir of the steamboat era on the Mississippi River before the Civil War. The Mississippi River and the Mississippi Delta, which Twain discusses, are geographical features that have been vital to the formation of the blues.

Richie Unterberger, "The Blues as Folklore," in *All Music Guide to the Blues*. 3rd ed. Ed. Vladimir Bogdanov, Chris Woodstra, and Stephen Thomas Erlewine. San Francisco: Backbeat Books, 2003.

Michael Urban, *Russia Gets the Blues: Music, Culture, and Community in Unsettled Times*. Ithaca, NY: Cornell University Press, 2004. This book explores the music, culture, and community of the blues within post-Communist Russia.

Gayle Dean Wardlow, *Chasin' That Devil Music: Searching for the Blues*. San Francisco: Miller Freeman, 1998. This history of the blues is based on the author's collection of firsthand interviews, public records, and other documents, gathered over a period of decades. Includes portraits of famous and little-known blues musicians. Includes companion CD with over a dozen rare Delta blues recordings.

Periodicals and Newspapers

Russell Banks, "The Devil and Robert Johnson: The Blues and the 1990s," *New Republic,* April 29, 1991.

Etienne Bours and Alberto Nogueira, "The Birth of the Blues," *UNESCO Courier,* March 1991.

Rick Bragg, "The Blues Is Dying in the Place It Was Born," *New York Times,* April 22, 2001.

Kirsten A. Conover, "Singing the Blues: America's Original Folk Art That Celebrates the Triumph of the Spirit Is Now More Popular than Ever," *Christian Science Monitor,* November 21, 1996.

Douglas Henry Daniels, "The Significance of the Blues for American History," *Journal of Negro History,* Winter/Spring 1985.

Economist, "Rebirth of the Blues," May 4, 1996.

Marta J. Effinger, "The Struggle and the Dream," *Footsteps,* March/April 2002.

David Evans, "Editor's Introduction," *Black Music Research Journal,* Spring 2000, p. 1.

Fred J. Hay, "The Sacred/Profane Dialectic in Delta Blues: The Life and Lyrics of Sonny Boy Williamson," *Phylon,* vol. 48, no. 4 (1987).

Langston Hughes, "Songs called the Blues," *Phylon,* vol. 36, no. 2 (1941).

Joy Bennett Kinnon, "Are Whites Taking or Are Blacks Giving Away the Blues?" *Ebony,* September 1997.

Daniel Lieberfeld, "Million-Dollar Juke Joint: Commodifying Blues Culture," *African American Review,* Summer 1995.

Chris Morris, "Messin' with the Blues," *Billboard,* June 15, 1996.

Hiram Nall, "From Down South to Up South: An Examination of Geography in the Blues," *Midwest Quarterly,* Spring 2001.

Richard Newman, "A Tradition Begins," *Footsteps,* March/April 2002.

Harriet Ottenheimer, "The Blues Tradition in St. Louis," *Black Music Research Journal,* Autumn 1989.

Jon Pareles, "Is It Happy Birthday for the Blues?" *New York Times,* September 21, 2003.

Joel Selvin, "The Blues Tells Its Own Story," *San Francisco Chronicle,* September 20, 2003.

Jon Michael Spencer, "The Diminishing Rural Reside of Folklore in City and Urban Blues, Chicago 1915–1950," *Black Music Research Journal,* Spring 1992.

Jess Tyehimba, "The Word/The Blues. A Meditation. Investigating Blues Poetry, an Oral Tradition," *Black Issues Book Review,* March/April 2004.

Charles Whitaker, "Are Blacks Giving Away the Blues? White Fans Keep the Music and Its Artists Going Strong," *Ebony,* October 1990.

Video

The Blues, a Musical Journey, part 1: *Feel Like Goin' Home.* Produced and directed by Martin Scorsese. New York: Sony Music Entertainment/Columbia Music Video, 2003. Using performance, historical documentation, and interviews, this documentary explores the African roots of American blues and the importance the blues plays in the historical and racial identity of African Americans.

The Blues: A Musical Journey, part 3: *Road to Memphis.* Produced and directed by Richard Pearce. New York: Sony Music Entertainment Columbia Music Video, 2003. This documentary traces the musical odyssey of blues legend B.B. King in a film that pays tribute to the great blues city, Memphis, Tennessee.

The Blues: A Musical Journey, part 5: *Godfathers and Sons.* Produced and directed by Marc Levin. New York: Sony Music Entertainment/Columbia Music Video, 2003. Using archival footage and never-before-seen performances, this film explores the heyday of Chicago blues as former Chicago blues musicians unite to produce an album that seeks to bring veteran blues players together with contemporary hip-hop musicians.

The Blues: A Musical Journey, part 6: *Red, White, and Blues.* Produced and directed by Mike Figgis. New York: Sony Music Entertainment/Columbia Music Video, 2003. Using interviews and historical footage, this film describes and examines the influence of American blues on British music during the 1950s and 1960s and the revival of the blues brought about by the British Invasion of the 1960s.

The Blues: A Musical Journey, part 7: *Piano Blues.* Produced and directed by Clint Eastwood. New York: Sony Music Entertainment/Columbia Music Video, 2003. Using interviews, contemporary and historic performances, and historical footage, this documentary traces the history and discusses the importance of the piano in American blues.

Blues Like Showers of Rain. Produced and directed by John Jeremy. Lyme, CT: Rhapsody Films, 1986. This video explores the early origins of the blues in rural, black, southern communities, primarily in the Mississippi Delta and in Texas.

Chicago Blues. Produced and directed by Harley Cokliss. Lyme, CT: Rhapsody Films, 1991. Traces the evolution of blues music from its origins in the rural south and focuses on its development in the urban environment of Chicago. Includes performances by Muddy Waters and others.

Essential Blues Masters History of the Blues, Volume 1. Written by Barbara L. Kaye. Directed by L.L. Tarter. Los Angeles: Rhino Home Video, 1993. Using rare performance recordings and historical footage, this documentary traces the history of the blues.

Land Where the Blues Began. Produced by Alan Lomax. New York: Phoenix Films, 1980. This documentary about Mississippi blues and life traces the origins of the music using documentation, recordings, and interviews with Mississippi blues players and residents.

Rise and Fall of Jim Crow. Program 1, *Promises Betrayed.* Produced by Sam Pollard. San Francisco: California Newsreel, 2002. This series examines the rise of racist segregation laws from the post–Civil War period through the civil rights era.

Audio Recordings

Jimpson & ax gang, "No More, My Lord," *Prison Songs.* Vol. 1, *Murderous Home.* Green Records, 1997.

Web Sites

Heavenly Midis Songbook (http://my. homewithgod.com/heavenlymidis/ songbook/index.html). This online songbook contains the lyrics to many religious songs, including spirituals.

Delta Blues Museum (www.deltablues museum.org). This site includes historical and current information about the Mississippi Delta and the music called the Delta blues.

American Studies Department, University of Virginia (http://xroads. virginia.edu/~ma02/easton/vaudeville/vaudeville.html). "Vaudeville! A History." This site includes historical essays, audio, and video describing, examining, and portraying the art of vaudeville.

Internet Sources

Alan Coukell, "Etta Baker, Legend of Piedmont Blues," NPR, March 16, 2005. www.npr.org/templates/story/ story.php?storyId=4536802.

George Gibson, "Gourd Banjos: From Africa to the Appalachians," Gourd Banjo Web site. www.dhyatt.com/ history_3_colamer.html.

Max Hymes, "Blues Definitions," Early Blues Web site. www.earlyblues. com/Blues_definitions.htm.

• Index •

Hay, Fred J., 71
Haymes, Max, 11
Healer, The (record album), 89
Helena, Arkansas, 57, 58
"High Sheriff Blues" (song), 40
hip-hop music, 11, 94
Hohner, Matthias, 30
Hoodoo cult. See voodoo
Hooker, John Lee, 64, 89, 90
Hopkins, Lightnin', 69, 85, 92
horns, 16–18, 46, 64
House, Son, 40, 50, 51, 52, 53, 77
House of Blues, 90
Howlin' Wolf, 40, 59, 74, 78
Hughes, Langston, 10, 49
humor, 36
Hunter, Alberta, 50
Hurt, Mississippi John, 76, 77

Iglauer, Bruce, 91
international blues, 74–75, 81–82
Internet, the, 91

Jackson, Michael, 84
James, Elmore, 59
James, Etta, 84, 87
James, Skip, 40, 50, 76, 77, 78
jazz
    classic female blues and, 43, 44
    Harlem and, 49
    influence of blues on, 11, 61
    jump blues and, 64
    New Orleans and, 18
Jefferson, Blind Lemon, 33, 39, 41, 50, 51
Jefferson, Thomas, 16
Jewish people, 62
Jim Crow laws, 24–25
John Henry ballads, 22–23
John Mayall's Bluesbreakers (band), 78, 82
Johnson, Lyndon B., 71
Johnson, Robert, 38, 40, 53, 63, 89, 93
Johnson, Tommy, 38, 53, 93
Joplin, Janis, 76
Joplin, Scott, 42
Jordan, Louis, 64
jug bands, 60
jukeboxes, 55–56
juke joints, 56, 57
jump blues, 46, 54, 64–65
jump-ups, 20

KFFA (radio station), 57, 58
King, B.B., 73–74
    on black heritage, 86–87
    on the blues, 9
    influence of, 78
    music industry and, 90
    radio programs and, 57, 59

urban blues and, 69
white audiences and, 68, 78
King, Chris Thomas, 93
King, Martin Luther, Jr., 71
King Biscuit Entertainers (band), 58
King Biscuit Time (radio program), 57, 58
Kings of Rhythm (band), 67
Kinnon, Joy Bennett, 84
Knight, Gladys, 72
Koda, Cub, 46
Korner, Alex, 74
Ku Klux Klan (KKK), 25
KWEM (radio station), 59

languages, African, 18
Latin America, slaves in, 15
law enforcement, 39–40, 58
Leadbelly, 33, 52
Ledbetter, Huddie, 33, 52
Led Zeppelin (band), 78
Legba (voodoo god), 38
Lewis, Furry, 77
Lewis, Jerry Lee, 55
Library of Congress, 52
Lieberfeld, Daniel, 90
Life on the Mississippi (Twain), 28
"Like a Rollin' Stone" (song), 76
Little Boy Blue, 58
Little Richard, 73
Lockwood, Robert, Jr., 58
Lomax, Alan, 52
    on emotional expression, 11, 34, 36
    on jukeboxes, 56
    on the Mississippi Delta, 29
    on popularity of the blues, 78
Lomax, John A., 52
Louisiana Purchase, 13
lutes, 16
lyrics, 33–34, 36, 40, 65

Mayall, John, 78, 82
Mayfield, Percy, 64
Memphis, Tennessee, 60
"Memphis Blues" (song), 42
Memphis Minnie, 63
Memphis Recording Service. *See* Sun Records
"Messin' with the Kid" (song), 91
Mexican music, influence of, 33
Miller, Willie, 58
Milteau, J.J., 82
Mississippi Delta, 27–28, 87
    see also Delta blues
Mississippi River flood (1927), 37
Montgomery bus boycott, 71
Moody Blues, the (band), 75
Morganfield, McKinley. See Muddy Waters
Morris, Chris, 89
Morton, Jelly Roll, 48–49

• Picture Credits •

• About the Author •

Andy Koopmans is a writer and amateur blues musician living in Seattle,
Washington. This is his fourteenth book.

He would like to thank everyone at Lucent Books, particularly editor Jen-
nifer Skancke and production editor Ryan Smith, for their help in preparing
this book for publication.